THE REFRACTIVE THINKER®

AN ANTHOLOGY OF DOCTORAL WRITERS

VOLUME VI

Post-Secondary Education

Edited by Dr. Cheryl A. Lentz

THE REFRACTIVE THINKER® PRESS

The Refractive Thinker®: An Anthology of Higher Learning

The Refractive Thinker® Press
9065 Big Plantation Avenue
Las Vegas, NV 89143-5440   USA

info@refractivethinker.com
www.refractivethinker.com

Books are available through The Refractive Thinker® Press at special discounts for bulk purchases for the purpose of sales promotion, seminar attendance, or educational purposes. Special volumes can be created for specific purposes and to organizational specifications. Please contact us for further details.

Individual authors own the copyright to their individual materials.
The Refractive Thinker® Press has each author's permission to reprint.

Orders placed on www.refractivethinker.com for students and military receive a 15% discount. We support the USO.

Copyright © 2011 by The Refractive Thinker® Press
Managing Editor: Dr. Cheryl A. Lentz

Library of Congress Control Number: 2011929140

Volume ISBNs	Soft Cover	978-0-9828740-8-0
	E-book/PDF	978-0-9828740-9-7
	*Kindle and electronic versions available	

Refractive Thinker® logo by Joey Root, The Refractive Thinker® Press logo design by Jacqueline Teng, cover design by Peri Poloni-Gabriel, Knockout Design, www.knockoutbooks.com, final production by Gary A. Rosenberg, www.garyarosenberg.com.

Printed in the United States of America

10   9   8   7   6   5   4   3   2   1

Contents

FOREWORD
Jonathan A. Kaplan, vii

Preface, ix

Acknowledgments, xi

"The whole purpose of education is to turn mirrors into windows."

—Sydney J. Harris

Foreword

I write this at a time when we have lost one of the world's most famous refractive thinkers—Apple visionary and CEO Steve Jobs. Along the lines of Henry Ford or Thomas Edison, Jobs was able to seemingly peer into the future and determine what we as consumers wanted even before we knew ourselves. His legacy of technology breakthroughs truly revolutionized how we live and work; yet it is his creative mindset, his ability to 'think different', as the famous Apple motto says, that perhaps leaves us with an even greater and more enriching gift.

It is fitting that we ask what lessons we may learn from Jobs as we dedicate this issue of *The Refractive Thinker*® to exploring the future of post-secondary education. Jobs did not follow a single path of education. In fact, he never graduated college. But Jobs was an active consumer of education, and he audited classes that met his own personal interests and passions. And it was from some of the most unexpected places that he drew his most valuable insights. For instance, he credited a calligraphy course for inspiring multiple typefaces for the future Macintosh computer. Imagine being limited to one font today. Jobs couldn't . . . and he didn't.

I am no Steve Jobs. Yet, as president of Walden University, I'm required to ask others to put aside their own ideas and preconceptions of a single path in postsecondary education and consider alternate routes. Although this is difficult for some, it is necessary and essential if we as higher education leaders are to provide greater access to educational opportunities for all adult learners.

Much has been written about the growing educational gap in our country, and if we are to meet the demands for college graduates, we must begin to 'think different'. How does higher education fit in the lives of working adults? How do we reach out to multiple styles of learners? And how do we provide them with curriculum that is relevant and practical to the 21st century workplace? You'll discover what some of today's thought leaders have to say about these topics in this issue.

To be a refractive thinker is to be willing to put aside old paradigms and push established boundaries. It is a difficult thing to do, particularly in education, but it can be done. I think back to Walden's own beginnings more than 40 years ago. It was a trio of educators, and refractive thinkers in their own right, who dared to ask: "What if students were placed at the center of the educational experience?" Subsequently Walden was founded to offer working adults the opportunity to pursue their doctoral degrees through the flexibility of distance learning. Today, Walden continues that spirit of innovation, looking at new ways to improve our students' learning experience because we know good teaching can come in many forms and functions.

I encourage you to use this issue of *The Refractive Thinker®* as an opportunity to consider news paths for the future of higher education. You may discover, as Steve Jobs illustrated for all us, that sometimes a path can lead us to an entire new world. It is a challenging time for education, but not an impossible one, if we choose to 'think different'.

Jonathan A. Kaplan
President, Walden University

Preface

I am a Refractive Thinker.

Welcome to The Refractive Thinker®
Vol VI: Post-Secondary Education

Thank you for joining us for the Fall 2011 edition, as we continue to celebrate the accomplishments of doctoral educators affiliated with many phenomenal institutions of higher learning. The purpose of this offering within this award winning anthology series is to continue adding to the collective discussion specifically on the topic of post-secondary education. Our goal is to dig deeper, examining the current state of higher education as it evolves, while shaping the lives of administrators, faculty, and the students these institutions serve.

This peer-reviewed resource presents scholarly discourse from multiple authors within the chapters that follow, each offering their unique perspective, experience, and expertise. Further, these approaches reflect the construct of the refractive thinker where each author challenges the conventional wisdom to expand beyond traditional boundaries and limits. These authors dared to not just think outside of the box, but to bend thought in unexpected ways to further discussion by challenging the old, while contemplating and debating future possibilities. Instead of merely settling for what *is,* these authors intentionally strive to push and test limits considering what *could be.*

Please contact The Refractive Thinker® Press for further information regarding these authors and the works contained within these pages. Perhaps you or your organization may be looking for their expertise to incorporate as part of your annual corporate meetings as a keynote or guest speaker(s), or to offer individual or group seminars, coaching, or consultation.

We look forward to your interest in discussing future opportunities. Come join us in our quest to be refractive thinkers and add your wisdom to the collective. We look forward to your stories.

Acknowledgments

The foundation of leadership embraces the art of asking questions—to validate and affirm *what* we do and *why*. Leaders often challenge this status quo, to offer alternatives and new directions, to dare to try something that has not yet been done as again proved true in this case with our second edition of Volume VI. This publication required the continued belief in this new publishing model by those willing to continue forward on this voyage. As a result, please let me express my gratitude for the help of the many that made this project possible.

First, let me offer a special thank you to Trish Hladek for her unwavering support and belief that traversing unchartered waters is worthy of the journey. My gratitude extends to our Peer Review Board to include: Dr. Laura Grandgenett and Dr. Judy Blando; and our Board of Directors to include: Dr. Judy Fisher-Blando, Dr. Tom Woodruff, (and myself), and our Author Advisory Board Dr. Sheila Embry. In addition, let me offer a well deserved thank you to our production specialist, Gary Rosenberg; Refractive Thinker® logo designer, Joey Root; and our cover designer, Peri Poloni-Gabriel, Knockout Design, and companion website designer, Jacqueline Teng, maintained by AJ Shope.

Let me also extend my sincere gratitude to all participating authors within The Refractive Thinker® series who continue to believe in this project as we continue to expand our program. We appreciate their commitment to leadership and to the concept of what it means to be a refractive thinker.

Dr. Cheryl A. Lentz
Managing Editor
Las Vegas, NV
November 2011

THE REFRACTIVE THINKER®

Retaining and Graduating Adult Students in Higher Education: Using Learning Styles to Increase Student Success

Dr. Elena Murphy

The U.S. Department of Education projected that by 2014, approximately eight million adult students, 25 and older will be actively enrolled in some type of degree-granting post-secondary education (National Center for Education Statistics, 2006). Although college administrators observe a trend in rising enrollment for adult students, administrators are still faced with the issue of students who drop out of school before completing a degree. Consequently, student departure before completing a degree is a problem that negatively affects the finances of the higher education institution (Bodfish, 2002).

Administrators in higher education institutions are accountable to the accrediting agencies that look at graduation rates to monitor school performance and become concerned with excessive student departure. Federal agencies and state education departments measure accountability at colleges and universities by monitoring reported student graduation rates (Goenner & Snaith, 2004). According to Levitz, Noel, and Richter (1999), graduation rates are one of the key performance indicators institutions of higher learning use to measure colleges' and universities' accountability, while retention is used by educational administrators as an institutional performance indicator, measured by observing "student satisfaction and success" (p. 31).

Student retention efforts are the responsibility of the higher education administration, faculty, and staff (Powell, 2003). Educational leaders become concerned when there is an indication of high attrition rates, suggesting a need to examine program processes, curriculum delivery methods, or student support services within the institution. To make improvements toward increasing student retention, educational leaders need to be aware of the factors that influence a student's decision to complete a degree and why students depart from the college program without finishing their degree (Summers, 2003).

Educational leaders and faculty can contribute to student persistence by offering a variety of institutional support that will help retain students. Lau (2003) suggested that educational leaders can offer scholarships and academic assistance, and faculty can use innovative instructional techniques to help students be successful as defined by the ability to graduate from a program of study. Jarrell (2004) supported the notion that to increase student persistence, institutional systems need to be in place that support the success of the student in the academic environment. While the previous studies on persistence conducted by Lau (2003) and Jarrell (2004) are useful for understanding college student persistence, the studies focused on traditional-aged students and freshmen retention results and neglected the adult student population.

Research studies on traditional-age students and the role of learning styles and retention of these college students abound. The findings of the research have shown that faculty knowledge of students' learning styles is beneficial to students' academic success in college courses (Diaz & Cartnal, 1999; Felder &

Brent, 2005; Healy & Jenkins, 2000; Jones, Reichard, & Mokhtari, 2003), classroom environments (Aragon, Johnson, & Shaik 2002; Fahy & Mohamed, 2005; Garland & Martin, 2005), and university attendance (Clump & Skogsberg, 2003; Dunn & Griggs, 2000). Additional studies are needed in the area of learning styles and its effect on retaining adult students specifically in adult bachelor's degree completion programs.

Working adult students enrolled in college require an accessible degree program provided in a manner that will accommodate life obligations such as family, work, and limited free time (Lumina Foundation, 2005). Colleges and universities face the challenge of addressing the time and convenience issues of adult students by offering evening courses and weekend accelerated programs that shorten the length of time for an adult student to obtain a degree. Traditional college degree programs require students to enroll full-time and attend daytime courses, which is not conducive to the needs of working adult students. Educational leaders and faculty have modified traditional daytime courses and degree offerings to meet the needs of adult commuting students who take courses at night and on weekends (Maehl, 2004).

With the increase of adult student enrollment on college campuses, the administrators and faculty are challenged to address the academic learning needs of the older population (Kalin & Shafto, 2004; Maehl, 2004; Noel-Levitz, 2005). In the mid-1990s, college and university administrators saw an opportunity to attract and enroll an underserved population of adult learners to the campus as well as create new tuition revenue. Adult bachelor degree completion programs on traditional college and university campuses were developed to meet the learning needs of the enrolled adult students (Maehl, 2004).

Specific degree programs catering to adult learners were

designed to offer students the flexibility, convenience, and accelerated format for obtaining a bachelor's degree. When educational leaders consider these factors for accommodating adult learners, students are more likely to enroll in a college degree program (Lumina Foundation, 2010). The main objective for college administrators is to increase enrollment on campus and retain the enrolled students until graduation.

Retaining adult students until graduation is an important issue for educational leaders to consider because the enrollment of adult students adds to the revenue stream of the college (Maehl, 2004; Noel-Levitz, 2005). Tuition-driven private colleges and universities rely on student revenue to operate the school (Summers, 2003). Student tuition is counted within the revenue projections and operating budgets determined prior to the start of the school year (Odden & Piccus, 2004). Pressure is on the school administrators and faculty to meet the budget by retaining the registered students in the program until graduation (Moll, 1994). Focusing on the adult student population offers colleges and universities an alternative revenue stream that brings additional income into the college rather than relying exclusively on the income from traditional-age student enrollment (Maehl, 2004).

One way educational leaders and faculty can improve student retention is by understanding learning style types as part of a student's enrollment profile and characteristics for academic success and persistence in college (Healey & Jenkins, 2000; Terry, 2001; Yorke, 2004). Higher education faculty can benefit from recognizing that adults enrolling in a degree program bring different learning style preferences to the classroom. Faculty can make teaching modifications to the learning environment that may bring about greater efficiency in both teaching and learning success (Sims & Sims, 1995).

Attrition Research

Student retention and attrition are important issues of concern for educational administrators and faculty. Because more adults are entering higher education, studies are reflecting the need to research the retention and attrition habits of the adult population (Bean & Metzner, 1985; Kerka, 1997; Nippert, 2000). According to the Lumina Foundation (2010), 40% of adult students over the age of 25 were participating in some form of post-secondary education. Despite this trend of adult learners enrolling in degree programs, researchers generally have conducted studies focusing on the characteristics of the traditional-age student population to explain the attrition phenomenon. Various factors such as age (Astin, 1975; Pascarella & Terenzini, 2005), gender (Huang, Taddese, & Walter, 2000), and ethnicity (Wilds & Wilson, 1998), have been researched and used to explain why traditional student departure occurs in colleges and universities. Factors could be internal or psychological, such as sense of community, lack of institutional integration, or lack of commitment, or they could be external factors, such as societal and environmental influences (Tinto, 1993).

Educational administrators face the conundrum of identifying the type of attrition that is occurring in their institution. College administrators may not know why a student drops out of college before completing a degree. In a study by Schuetz (2005), research indicated that 40% of student populations dropping from a community college impede institutions from identifying whether students are considered as dropping out from the system, taking a break, or transferring to another college. Hoyt and Winn (2004) in their study provided an explanation of diverse student subpopulations indicated by the terms drop-out, transfer-out, and stop-out. Students can drop-out from an academic program and never return to higher education; or they can transfer-out and leave an institution to seek a better education at a different institution; or they can temporarily stop-out of a program of study with the intention to return to the institution later.

Hoyt and Winn (2004) explored the differences between students who drop-out, transfer-out, and stop-out to determine the reasons the students left before completing a program of study. Results from the study identified varying factors affecting the decisions of students to leave the institution. According to Hoyt and Winn (2004), drop-out and stop-out students tended to be "older than 25 years of age, have children, and conflicts with job responsibilities" (p. 403). In contrast, the researchers observed that transfer-out students tended to be 20 years of age, have parental support, and no children (p. 404).

In a different study looking at the risk factors on student retention in higher education, Hoyt and Lundell (2004) had similar results indicating that, "Part-time and older students, single parents, and students with children have substantially higher attrition rates. International students also have high dropout rates" (p. 6). Looking at the factors that effected student retention provided institutions with a means to decide on a plan of action to remedy the situation. One recommendation of the study supported the idea of educational institutions implementing a student services intervention program to identify and assist at risk students before they drop out of a college program.

Consequently, in an article addressing the retention problem in higher education, Barefoot (2004) identified institutions that have developed retention programs based on research data and discovered a correlation between traditional-age student retention and college involvement. However, Barefoot indicated that while the programs have been useful for academically assisting the traditional-aged college students' experience, the program did not notably benefit adult learners and working students. Adult students furthering their education have difficulty integrating into the traditional campus environment, especially if they are attending classes in the evenings and commuting to the campus.

In a qualitative case study conducted by Monroe (2006), one nontraditional transfer student's college experience was explored. The conclusion drawn from the case study indicated that the student had difficulty navigating the institutional system and the institution lacked the support to assist the student effectively in her integration into the program. While Monroe's study is meaningful in adding to the body of literature on nontraditional student attrition, the case study reflected the departure pattern of one older female student and her interaction at a single institution and does not necessarily reflect the total adult student body attending the college.

A more general study was conducted by Golde (2005) who performed a qualitative study exploring the function and services of higher education personnel in relation to doctoral student attrition to determine an institutional influence on why students leave college before completing a degree. The findings imply that a culture projected by particular academic departments can influence the integration of students in a doctoral program and can affect whether a student stays or leaves school prior to degree completion. Golde (2005) suggested that while this study focused on four departments at one university, the findings might not be generalizable to other institutions.

While the above studies addressed student specific issues, Ishitani and DesJardins (2002) conducted a multi-institutional longitudinal study investigating student drop-out behavior over a 5-year period. The results of the study indicated that financial aid had a large influence on whether a student stayed or departed college. Disadvantaged and minority student dropout rates increased when problems arose with financial issues.

Further examinations of higher education institutions by Braxton and Mundy (2001) addressed the problem of student attrition and found that institutional leaders could not eliminate attrition by having one sweeping policy that covered all students. Braxton and Mundy suggested that institutional administrators develop many small policy levers that can address the variety of attrition variables identified by the particular college or university. For example, levers can be implemented that assist students with the task of navigating the campus system, providing assistance through faculty advisement, and offering assessment testing that can help students integrate into the campus environment (Braxton & Mundy, 2001).

Although studies have examined attrition for its causes and prevention, the problem remains with specifically identifying variables that would be generalizable to all students on all campuses. The factors that contribute to attrition on one campus may not explain the factors for other campuses. Administrators face the challenge of developing retention programs that will meet the needs of adult students. Each student is different, and the reasons that cause one student to leave could be very different for another student. Gaps in literature concerning retention and attrition rates among adult students attending degree completion programs are of interest to administrators and faculty in setting policy and making curriculum improvements (Donaldson & Graham, 2001). Gaps also are apparent in the literature with the paucity of studies that examined the graduation rate of adult nontraditional students, specifically from adult degree completion programs.

Learning Styles Research and Student Success

Learning style research in relation to student academic achievement and success in the classroom can offer benefits to the faculty in that instructional methods can be modified based on students' learning preferences. Dunn, Griggs, Olson, Gorman, and Beasley (1995) investigated learning styles and student achievement of more than 3,100 students through a meta-analysis of 42 studies to determine the validation of the model of learning style preferences. The results of the Dunn et al. (1995) meta-analysis indicated that when students' learning styles are congruent with instructional methods, student achievement increased as much as 75% over students whose learning styles did not match instructional methods. Dunn et al. also found that adult and post-secondary students demonstrated increased gains in academic success compared with secondary level students when instructional interventions and learning styles were matched. Studies have also found that students who are aware of their learning style are more likely to adjust their style to meet their learning needs (Dunn & Griggs, 2000; Kolb & Kolb, 2005).

Students who have knowledge of their own learning styles were more successful in the learning environment. Schatteman, Carette, Couder, and Eisendrath (1997) examined learning style as a separate variable among others to determine an increase in student performance in the classroom. Schatteman et al. (1997) found that students' knowledge of their own style of learning helped them achieve better grades; in addition, teachers adapting instruction to help students effectively use learning styles contributed to the learning process for students. Faculty who understand the concept of learning style in teaching and purposely use the knowledge can create course curriculum conducive to a multitude of learning styles (Nicholls, 2002). The faculty can enhance the learning process through the effective design of course materials, lectures, and adjustment to teaching style as well.

Similarly, another study identified a connection between awareness of educators' teaching styles and students' learning styles. Charkins, O'Toole, and Wetzel (1985) outlined the findings of a prior ex post facto study conducted at Purdue University in 1982 using the Grasha-Reichmann Learning Styles Questionnaire with 600 students and 20 teachers. The findings indicated a link between learning and teaching styles in the classroom. Charkins et al. (1985) found that the larger the discrepancy between the teacher's preferred style of teaching and the student's preferred style of learning, produced lower achievement results in students. College faculty can use learning styles research to adjust teaching styles to accommodate instruction and produce effective student learning outcomes while meeting the variety of learning style preferences encountered in the classroom (Charkins et al., 1985).

Students can adjust their learning styles as they become more aware of a teacher's teaching style to increase success in learning. In a study by Cano-Garcia and Hughes (2000) more than 200 college students learning styles and thinking styles were compared to determine if the styles had any relationship to, or influence on academic achievement. Cano-Garcia and Hughes used Kolb's Learning Style Inventory as one of two instruments in the study. One finding from the research found that students who adapted their own learning style in the classroom to fit the instructional teaching style received better marks. The second finding showed that the classroom environment was instructionally enriched when faculty made a concerted effort to understand their students' learning styles and planned curriculum accordingly.

Students acknowledging learning styles and confidently using learning style preferences when performing class activities see improved achievement. Cassidy and Eachus (2000) conducted a study that identified the significant factors of learning styles and academic belief systems in college students taking a research methods course. The study found that academic achievement was impacted by learning style and student confidence when attempting a task. They saw learning style as an integration of how students plan strategic approaches to learning. When accommodations were self-imposed, the students did better in learning the information taught by the faculty.

In a study by Manochehri and Young (2006) comparing the effect of learning style preferences of students in two different learning environments, significance was demonstrated in preferred styles and knowledge acquisition. Kolb's Learning Style Inventory instrument was used to collect data from the undergraduate students using the four learning styles of Converger, Assimilator, Accommodator, and Diverger. The study examined learning styles effect on the dependent variables of knowledge acquisition and student satisfaction in both online learning and traditional classroom learning.

The researchers found a statistical significance in knowledge acquisition based on learning styles, especially in the online environment when compared to regular classroom learning (Manochehri & Young, 2006). Students who demonstrated Kolb's Assimilator and Converger learning styles increased performance in the web-based learning environment (Manochehri & Young, 2006). The styles indicated were consistent with Kolb's theory that the Converger type preferred technology and the Assimilator type preferred concise theoretical information presented in an organized and logical manner.

In a study conducted by Moores, Change, and Smith (2004) on experiential learning styles and class performance of undergraduate students, the findings showed that students attending a technology related course demonstrated a high correlation between the learning mode of abstract concept and course grade performance. Students' using the learning mode of abstract concepts is preferable in an Information Systems course as logical analysis is an important factor in applying and designing computer related systems (Moores et al., 2004). The implications of these findings suggest that faculty using learning styles developed from the theory of experiential learning can create course material specific to the learning mode strength of the students while also challenging students to exercise the weaker learning modes (Moores et al., 2004).

Student learning outcomes have become a major focus of state education departments, especially concerning accreditation issues confronting colleges and universities (Ratcliff, Lubinescu, & Gaffney, 2001). Student learning outcomes are measured by college faculty through various types of assessment testing such as faculty-developed multiple-choice tests, essay tests, portfolios demonstrating student work, and assigned projects. From the assessment results, faculty determine if students have been successful in learning the information delivered in the classroom.

While student learning outcomes are an important factor for demonstrating achievement, Kolb and Kolb (2005) indicated that faculty should focus more on the *process* of learning rather than on the *outcomes*. The learning process is an active engagement of students in the examination of what they are thinking while the learning is occurring. Students continually construct knowledge from new learning by reviewing the learning and understanding the fit with the schema of the previous knowledge learned.

When an educator helps students to recognize how learning styles are used, the student becomes aware of the conflict occurring between what is known and how the new information can be adapted in a student's mind as part of the learning process (Kolb & Kolb, 2005). Sutliff and Baldwin (2001) have shown that teachers who adjust their instruction based on student learning style preferences, raise the level of success in the learning environment. Faculty who consider the learning abilities of the students can modify the curriculum to meet the needs of the students in the class and improve student-learning acquisition.

Using Learning Styles in Higher Education

Student learning styles research is evident in the literature from studies on K-12 education up to post-secondary education (Claxton & Murrell, 1988; Dunn & Dunn, 1978; Sarasin, 1999). While learning style research has focused on elementary to post-secondary students, research is still needed on understanding the learning preferences of adult students for graduation success in higher education. Previous research studies exist focusing on recruitment, retention, and attrition of traditional-age students at community colleges and 4-year universities (Bean, 1982; Spady, 1970; Summers, 2003; Tinto, 1993), but have neglected including the adult learner attending bachelor degree completion programs in similar research.

The concept of learning styles and how an individual chooses to comprehend and process new information has notable theoretical foundations in the literature. Learning styles are a series of patterned actions that a student implements when encountering a learning environment, and these patterned actions govern the process of developing new abilities and acquiring knowledge (Sarasin, 1999). Individuals perform learning tasks using a preferred learning mode. Individuals can approach a task using cognitive learning styles, affective learning style, or physiological learning styles (Cassidy, 2004).

Cognitive style is described as a combination of emotions, behaviors, mental status, physiology, and the awareness of one's reactions to the present surroundings (Williams, Anshel, & Quek, 1997). An individual using a cognitive learning style uses brain-based thinking and processing while performing tasks and seeks an analytical approach to the experience (Sims & Sims, 1995). The physiological learning used by an individual has a biological-base relating to diet, fitness, and gender and their influence on an individual's knowledge acquisition ability (Sims & Sims, 1995). Consequently, the cognitive learning styles described are similar to Kolb's orientation of the individual using a concrete experience/abstract conceptualization adaptive mode for learning. In contrast, an individual using an affective learning style approaches tasks using intuition and self-perception to interpret experience to process the event. Likewise, the affective learning style can be compared to Kolb's active experimentation/reflective observation adaptive modes for learning. Kolb (1984) explained, "An affective environment emphasizes the experiencing of concrete events; a symbolic environment emphasizes abstract conceptualization; a perceptual environment stresses observation and appreciation; a behavioral environment stresses action taking in situations with real consequences" (p. 197). Faculty can intentionally create learning environments conducive to student learning through awareness of the different learning concepts.

Dunn and Dunn (1978) conducted extensive research exploring cognitive learning styles, especially in younger students, and developed the model of learning style preferences that has been used extensively by other researchers. From the study, Dunn and Dunn identified various learning style preferences among students in different subject areas and the preferred style that students use, thereby providing a means for teachers to assess and direct instruction for student learning success in the classroom. Student motivation and success at learning tasks increased when students' learning styles were considered in the teacher's instructional lesson (Dunn, Griggs, Olson, Gorman, & Beasley, 1995). Dunn et al. concluded using a learning style inventory to determine students' learning preferences can assist faculty in the classroom to increase student academic success.

In a study conducted by Murphy (2007), the Kolb Learning Style Inventory was used to determine learning style preferences and graduation success of adult students enrolled in a college's accelerated bachelor's program. Kolb's four learning style types of Accommodator, Assimilator, Converger, and Diverger were analyzed with the variable of student graduation. Archival student data were obtained for a total population of 3,504 adult students enrolled in a northeastern college from 1993 to 2005. A quantitative ex post facto correlational design methodology was employed to analyze the archival study data. Significant findings of the study indicated that there was a statistical difference between learning style types and graduation. Students with the Converger learning style type had a higher graduation likelihood compared with the other learning style types, while students with the Diverger learning style type were more likely to not complete the degree.

A Chi-square goodness of fit test was performed between the learning styles of Accommodator, Converger, Diverger, Assimilator and graduation (withdrawn or graduation). There was a difference found between the learning styles and graduation (withdrawn or graduation), $\chi^2 (3) = 80.034$, $p < .001$, such that those participants with learning style Diverger tended to have withdrawn more often than having graduated. Further analysis determined the graduation rate among enrollees exhibiting learning style Converger was the highest relative to graduation rates of enrollees with other learning styles. A logistic regression of graduation success and estimates for the four learning styles was performed. The strength of the significance of each learning style type was compared to the other three learning style types in a separate equation. Results indicated a high percentage difference for learning styles between those who graduated versus those who did not graduate. Students who had the Converger learning style were 80% more likely to graduate compared to students with the other learning style types. Conversely, students with the Diverger learning style type were 44% less likely to graduate compared to students with the other learning style types.

The results from the Murphy (2007) research study indicated learning style types and graduation provided useful information for educational leaders and faculty about the effect of student learning style preferences on degree completion. The findings of the study also contributed information toward the retention of adult students in a college's adult bachelor's degree completion program. Knowledge of the use of learning style types can assist faculty to adjust the program design, course outcomes, and classroom instruction for the purpose of improving retention (Claxton & Murrell, 1988). Research on learning style types and graduation success provides educational leaders with additional insight on whether student learning style type preferences can be used as one among many indictors used by colleges to determine a student's potential for success in an adult degree completion program.

Challenges facing faculty who teach adult students include discovering ways to assess the learning style types of enrolled students in the classroom (Sims & Sims, 1995). Educators can make students aware of their own learning style preferences by using a learning style instrument to help students discover preferred learning style types. In addition, a diagnostic learning style instrument to understand the learning preferences of adult students is useful for faculty in identifying the particular way students prefer to learn in the academic environment (Cambiano, Devore, & Denny, 2000; Yorke, 2004).

Faculty can use a variety of learning style instruments to obtain data for input in designing and modifying course curriculum and for accommodating the returning student in the classroom. Healey and Jenkins (2000) posited that personnel in higher education could benefit from examining the use of learning style types in the classroom to increase the retention rates of diverse students enrolled in college and university courses. Terry (2001) suggested that faculty at educational institutions can use learning styles as a predictor of student learning success, therefore improving the retention of students in the college.

Faculty can assist students with modifying and adjusting their own learning preferences by providing curriculum that requires students to process knowledge in a variety of ways. The instructor in the classroom can administer a learning style instrument at the beginning of the semester as part of the course instruction to help expand students' awareness of the different learning styles. By identifying learning style types and sharing the types in class, students become cognizant of the learning dimensions that are available for accommodating new information presented by the faculty. Sharing learning style types with students can increase the likelihood of students self-accommodating a faculty member's teaching style by shifting between learning styles preferences as needed (Dunn & Griggs, 2000).

Students who have a better understanding of how they prefer to receive and process new information are better able to adjust their styles depending on the circumstance (Kolb & Kolb, 2005). Consequently, Felder and Brent (2005) suggested that the objective of teachers knowing the learning styles of students provides opportunities for teachers to help students use a variety of learning style functions in different learning environments. Students proactively use the knowledge of learning preferences as a tool in various learning situations rather than the teacher just providing specific instruction to meet individual student learning style types.

Students bring into the classroom environment a preferred learning style type that can affect whether they will be successful in completing the program or drop out before graduating. Cassidy (2004) noted that learning predilection of students could influence student success and achievement. Learning style preferences have been shown to influence how students process new knowledge, thus effecting the outcome of students' learning success in the classroom (Honigsfeld & Dunn, 2006). Learning style research offers college administration and faculty an additional assessment tool for determining "individual differences while addressing learning" (Kolb, Boyatzis, & Mainemelis, 2001, p. 28) and for adjusting program curriculum to improve student success in higher education.

Conclusion

Retaining enrolled students in college is an important concern for many colleges and universities. As more adults are enrolling in degree-granting institutions, educational leaders need to seek ways to prevent student departure before graduation as students leaving college costs the institution a significant amount in revenue dollars (Swail, 2006). Student attrition and retention have long-term effects on colleges, especially if college administrators rely on students' tuition as a significant income source.

While there are many factors to explain why students depart before completing a degree, Tinto (2003) stated that administrators and faculty can increase student retention by creating an environment that is conducive to student success. One of the factors suggested was for faculty to look at the structure of the classroom environment and make accommodations in the classroom to promote student learning. Educators can collect information about students' learning styles preferences, skills, and abilities, and consider the information jointly for program and curriculum improvements to enhance student learning (Cambiano, Devore, & Denny, 2000; Palomba & Banta, 1999).

Faculty who have knowledge about students' learning style preferences can create a classroom environment that delivers instruction that reaches students who use a variety of learning modalities to process new information (Kolb, Boyatzis, & Mainemelis, 2001). By understanding students preferred style for approaching tasks and learning, faculty can specifically accommodate students through modifications of instructional design. For example, faculty can use technology in the classroom that can provide a means of visual, auditory, and kinesthetic instructional delivery modes that contribute to the different students' modality preferences for learning.

Educational leaders and faculty who emphasize the identification of students' learning styles within the classroom, are in alignment with research studies identifying learning styles as significantly correlated with student retention and graduation achievement (Cano-Garcia & Hughes, 2000; Cassidy & Eachus,

2000; Dunn & Griggs, 2000; Kasworm, Polson, & Fishback, 2002; Schatteman, Carette, Couder, & Eisendrath, 1997). Understanding adult students' learning style types is one of many factors that can be used to create a student profile that considers a holistic view of the student. Educators can better serve the students' needs in the classroom using a proactive measure like building a student profile and including learning styles to increase retention efforts and student success (Cassidy, 2004).

By making the accommodations based on the data collected from a student assessment, faculty can make decisions about curriculum delivery and instruction to necessitate the varying learning needs of students (Cambiano, Devore, & Denny, 2000). Consequently, faculty can focus and modify the curriculum for the adult learners as well by offering a classroom environment that is more learner-centered rather than teacher-centered (Schunk, 2004; Vella, 2002). A learner-centered environment can contain opportunities for students to apply theoretical knowledge through simulations and case studies while allowing the instructor to be a collaborator in the adult students' learning process.

REFERENCES

Aragon, S. R., Johnson, S. D., & Shaik, N. (2002). The influence of learning style preferences on student success in online versus face-to-face environments. *American Journal of Distance Education, 16*(4), 227–244.

Astin, A. W. (1975). *Preventing students from dropping out.* San Francisco, CA: Jossey-Bass.

Barefoot, B. (2004). Higher education's revolving door: Confronting the problem of student drop out in US colleges. *Open Learning, 19*(1), 9–18.

Bean, J. P. (1982). Student attrition, intentions, and confidence: Interaction effects in the path model. *Research in Higher Education, 17,* 291–319.

Bean, J. P., & Metzner, B. S. (1985). A conceptual model of nontraditional undergraduate student attrition. *Review of Educational Research, 55,* 485–540.

Bodfish, S. (2002). National enrollment management survey, 2001–2002. *Executive Summary.* Noel-Levitz, Inc. Retrieved from http://www.noel levitz.com/NR/rdonlyres/E63D7F22–64DF-4FF0-B685-E96F9E9 21FB4/0/2002_NEMS.pdf

Braxton, J. M., & Mundy, M. E. (2001). Powerful institutional levers to reduce college student departure. *Journal of College Student Retention, 3*(1), 91–118.

Cano-Garcia, F., & Hughes, E.H. (2000). Learning and thinking styles: An analysis of their interrelationship and influence on academic achievement. *Educational Psychology, 20*(4).

Cambiano, R. L., Devore, J. B., & Denny, G. S. (2000). Learning style preferences relating to adult students. *Academic Exchange Quarterly, 4*(2), 41.

Cassidy, S. (2004). Learning styles: An overview of theories, models, and measures. *Educational Psychology, 24*(4), 419–444.

Cassidy, S., & Eachus, P. (2000). Learning style, academic belief systems, self-report student proficiency, and academic achievement in higher education. *Educational Psychology, 20*(3), 307–322.

Charkins, R. J., O'Toole, D. M., & Wetzel, J. N. (1985). Linking teacher and student learning styles with student achievement and attitudes. *Journal of Economic Education, 16*(2), 111–120.

Claxton, C. S., & Murrell, P. H. (1988). *Learning styles.* Retrieved from http://www.ericdigests.org/pre-9210/learning.htm

Clump, M. A., & Skogsberg, K. (2003). Differences in learning styles of college students attending similar universities in different geographic locations. *College Student Journal, 37*(4), 501–508.

Diaz, D. P., & Cartnal, R. B. (1999). Students' learning styles in two classes. *College Teaching, 47*(4), 130–135.

Donaldson, J., & Graham, S. (2001, April). *Accelerated degree programs: Policy implications and critique.* Paper presented at the American Education Research Association National Conference in Seattle, Washington.

Dunn, R., & Dunn. K. (1978). *Teaching students through their individual learning styles: A practical approach.* Reston, VA: Reston Publishing Co.

Dunn, R., & Griggs, S. A. (Eds.). (2000). *Practical approaches to using learning styles in higher education.* Westport, CT: Bergin & Garvey Publishers.

Dunn, R., Griggs, S. A., Olson, J., Gorman, B., & Beasley, M. (1995). A meta-analytic validation of the Dunn and Dunn learning style model. *Journal of Educational Research, 88*(6), 353–361.

Fahy, P., & Mohamed, A. (2005). Student learning style and asynchronous computer-mediated conferencing (CMC) interaction. *American Journal of Distance Education, 19*(1), 5–22.

Felder, R. M., & Brent, R. (2005). Understanding student differences. *Journal of Engineering Education, 94*(1), 57–72.

Garland, D., & Martin, B. N. (2005). Do gender and learning style play a role in how online courses should be designed? *Journal of Interactive Online Learning, 4*(2), 67–81.

Goenner, C., & Snaith, S. (2004). Assessing the effects of increased admission standards. *College and University, 80*(1), 29–34.

Golde, C. M. (2005). The role of the department and discipline in doctoral student attrition: Lessons from four departments. *Journal of Higher Education, 76*(6), 669–700.

Healey, M. & Jenkins, A. (2000). Kolb's experiential learning theory and its application in geography in higher education. *Journal of Geography, 99*(5), 185–195.

Honigsfeld, A., & Dunn, R. (2006). Learning-style characteristics of adult learners. *The Delta Gamma Bulletin, 72*(2), 14–31.

Hoyt, J. E., & Lundell, M. (2004). *The effect of risk factors and student service interventions on college retention.* Retrieved from http://www.uvsc.edu/ir/research/Retentionwriteup.pdf

Hoyt, J. E., & Winn, B. A. (2004). Understanding retention and college student bodies: Differences between, drop-outs, stop-out, opt-outs, and transfer-outs. *NASPA, 41*(3), 395–417.

Huang, G., Taddese, N., & Walter, E. (2000). Entry and persistence of women and minorities in college science and engineering education. *Research and Development Report.* ERIC Document ED444872. Retrieved from http://eric.ed.gov/ERICWebPortal

Ishitani, T. T., & DesJardins, S. L. (2002). A longitudinal investigation of dropout from college in the United States. *Journal of College Student Retention, 4*(2), 173–201.

Jarrell, C. L. (2004). Creating a foundation for student success: From research to practice. *Community College Journal of Research and Practice, 28,* 513–524.

Jones, C., Reichard, C., & Mokhtari, K. (2003). Are students' learning styles discipline specific? *College Journal of Research and Practice, 27*(5), 363–375.

Kalin, C. J., & Shafto, S. A. (2004). *Enrollment management dynamics of adult undergraduate degree-completion business programs at private universities.* http://www.systemdynamics.org/conf2004/sds_2004/papers/315Kalin.pdf

Kasworm, C. E., Polson, C. J., & Fishback, S. J. (2002). *Responding to adult learners in higher education.* Malabar, FL: Krieger Publishing Company.

Kerka, S. (1997). Adult students and the college experience. *The Eric Review: Path to College 5*(3), 1–60. Retrieved from http://permanent.access.gpo.gov/lps50000/ERIC%20REVIEW%20ARCHIVE/vol5no3.pdf#search='The%20path%20to%20college%20Kerka'

Kolb, D. (1984). *Experiential learning: Experience as the source of learning and development.* Englewood Cliffs, NJ: Prentice-Hall.

Kolb, D. A., Boyatzis, R., & Mainemelis, C. (2001). *Experiential learning theory: Previous research and new directions.* In R. Sternberg and L. Zhang (Eds.). Perspectives on cognitive learning, and thinking styles. Mahwah, NJ: Lawrence Erlbaum Associates.

Kolb, A. Y., & Kolb, D. A. (2005). Learning styles and learning spaces: Enhancing experiential learning in higher education. *Academy of Management Learning and Education, 4*(2), 193–212.

Lau, L. K. (2003). Institutional factors affecting student retention. *Education, 124*(1), 126–136.

Levitz, R. S., Noel, L., & Richter, B. J. (1999). Strategic moves for retention success. *New Directions for Higher Education, 108,* 31–50.

Lumina Foundation. (2005). *What we know about access and success in post-secondary education.* Retrieved from http://www.luminafoundation.org/research/what_we_know/index.html

Lumina Foundation. (2010). *Request for proposals to increase adult degree completion.* Retrieved from http://www.luminafoundation.org

Maehl, W. H. (2004) Adult degrees and the learning society. *New Directions for Adult and Continuing Education,* (103), 5–16.

Manochehri, N., & Young, J. I. (2006). The impact of student learning styles with web-based learning or instructor-based learning on student knowledge and satisfaction. *The Quarterly Review of Distance Education, 7*(3), 313–316.

Moll, R. W. (1994). The scramble to get the new class. *Change, 26*(2).

Monroe, A. (2006). Non-traditional transfer student attrition. *The Community College Enterprise, 12*(2), 33–54.

Moores, T., Change, J., & Smith, D. (2004). Learning style and performance: A field study of IS students in an Analysis and Design course. *Journal of Computer Information Systems, 45*(1), 77–85.

Murphy, E. (2007). The relationship between learning styles and graduation among students in an adult degree completion program. Unpublished doctoral dissertation, University of Phoenix.

National Center for Education Statistics. (2006). *The condition of edu-*

cation 2006 (NCES 2006–071). U.S. Department of Education: Institute of Education Sciences. http://nces.ed.gov/pubsearch/pubsinfo.asp?pubid =2006071

Nicholls, G. (2002). *Developing teaching and learning in higher education.* New York, NY: Routledge Falmer.

Nippert, K. (2000). Influences on the educational degree attainment of two-year college students. *Journal of College Student Retention Research,* 2(1), 29–40.

Noel-Levitz, Inc. (2005). *The 2005 National Adult Student Priorities Report.* Retrieved from the Noel-Levitz, Inc. website. http://www.noel levitz.com/NR/rdonlyres/58C454FD-66A7–443E-82EC-DF72FE946 ADD/0/2005AdultSatisrpt.pdf

Odden, A. R., & Piccus, L. O. (2004). *School finance: A policy perspective* (3rd ed.). New York, NY: McGraw-Hill.

Palomba, C. A., & Banta, T. W. (1999). *Assessment essentials: Planning, implementing, and improving assessment in higher education.* Hoboken, NJ: John Wiley & Sons.

Pascarella, E. T., & Terenzini, P. T. (2005). *How college affects students: Findings and insights from twenty years of research: A third decade of research.* San Francisco, CA: Jossey-Bass.

Powell, T. (2003). New approach to curb low-retention rates. *Black Issues in Higher Education,* 20(18). Ratcliff, J. L., Lubinescu, E. S., & Gaffney, M. A. (Eds.). (2001). *How accreditation influences assessment.* New Directions for Higher Education, 113. San Francisco, CA: Jossey-Bass.

Sarasin, L. C. (1999). *Learning styles perspectives: Impact in the classroom.* Madison, WI: Atwood Publishing.

Schatteman, A., Carette E., Couder, J., & Eisendrath. H. (1997). Understanding the effects of a process-oriented instruction in the first year of a university by investigating learning style characteristics. *Educational Psychology, 17,* 111–125.

Schuetz, P. (2005). UCLA Community College review: Campus environment: A missing link in studies. *Community College Review,* 32(4), 60–80.

Schunk, D. H. (2004). *Learning theories: An educational perspective.* Upper Saddle River, NJ: Merrill Prentice-Hall.

ioncatEdu Education

Secondary Education

ary Education

Secondary Education

Secondary Education

Sims, R. R., & Sims, S. J. (Eds.). (1995). *The importance of learning styles: Understanding the implications for learning, course design, and education*. Westport, CT: Greenwood Press.

Spady, W. G. (1970). Dropouts from higher education: An interdisciplinary review and synthesis. *Interchange, 1*(1), 65–85.

Summers, M. D. (2003). ERIC review: Attrition research at community colleges. *Community College Review. 30*(4).

Sutliff, R. I., & Baldwin, V. (2001). Learning styles: Teaching technology subjects can be more effective. *The Journal of Technology Studies* [online journal] 22–27. Retrieved from http://scholar.lib.vt.edu/ejournals/JOTS/Winter-Spring-2001/sutliff.html

Swail, W. S. (2006). The art of student retention: A handbook for practitioners and administrators. *Educational Policy Institute*. Retrieved from http://www.educationalpolicy.org/pdf/ART.pdf

Terry, M. (2001). Translating learning style theory into university teaching practice: An article based on Kolb's Experiential Learning Model. *Journal of College Reading and Learning, 32*(1), 68–85.

Tinto, V. (1993). *Leaving college: Rethinking the causes and cures of student attrition* (2nd ed.). Chicago, IL: University of Chicago Press.

Tinto, V. (2003, November). *Promoting student retention through classroom practice.* Paper presented at an international conference sponsored by the European Access Network and the Institute for Access Studies at Staffordshire University, Amsterdam.

Vella, J. (2002). *Learning to listen learning to teach: The power of dialogue in educating adults*. San Francisco, CA: Jossey-Bass Publishers.

Wilds, D., & Wilson, R. (1998). *Minorities in higher education, 1997–1998: Sixteenth Annual Status Report*. Washington, DC: American Council on Education.

Williams, L. R., Anshel, M. H., & Quek, J. (1997). Cognitive style in adolescent competitive athletes as a function of culture and gender. *Journal of Sport Behavior, 20*(2), 232.

Yorke, M. (2004). Retention, persistence, and success in on-campus higher education. *Open Learning, 19*(1), 19–32.

About the Author

Dr. Elena Murphy holds a Bachelors of Science from SUNY Empire State College in Human Development; a Master of Science in Special Education from College of New Rochelle, and a Doctorate of Educational Leadership (Ed. D) from the University of Phoenix School of Advanced Studies.

Dr. Elena is faculty at a private northeastern college teaching and advising adult students in an accelerated bachelor's degree program. Dr. Elena also serves as a Thesis Advisor for graduate students in the Master of Science in Organizational Leadership program.

Dr. Elena has been working in the field of Prior Learning Assessment for the past 16 years. Previous publishing included a journal article for Journal of Continuing Higher Education.

Murphy, E. (2007). A review of Bloom's taxonomy and Kolb's theory of experiential learning: Practical uses for prior learning assessment. *Journal of Continuing Higher Education, 55*(3).

Dr. Elena has presented at conferences on the topics of prior learning and experiential learning.

Murphy, E., & Niner, N. (2001, November). *An effective approach to writing and assessing experiential learning.* Workshop presented at the Council for Adult and Experiential Learning (CAEL) Conference.

Murphy, E., & Dagavarian, D. (2005, November). *Marketing and financing prior learning assessment.* Workshop presented at the Council for Adult and Experiential Learning (CAEL) Conference.

Murphy, E., & Westerman, J. (2006, November). *Writing and assessing experiential learning essays using Kolb's learning theory.* Workshop presented at the Council for Adult and Experiential Learning (CAEL) Conference.

Dr. Elena is also an active member of the Council of Adult and Experiential Learning.

To reach Dr. Elena Murphy for potential writing collaboration projects, please send email to: DRMFACULTY@gmail.com

CHAPTER 2

Passion: Management Behavior to Build an Engaged Learning Mindset

Dr. Judy Fisher-Blando and Dr. Denise Land

Imagine an adult learning environment in which faculty brought effective practice of stewardship with a vision of engaging students in differentiated learning designed to maximize engagement with the learning process and student belief in their capacity to achieve high academic and knowledge-demonstration outcomes. Through a combined practice of servant and stewardship leadership practices, faculty can begin to set the stage upon which learning theory choreographed with student initiative and differentiated curriculum can make possible significant student outcomes. In an environment modified and supplemented toward student learning desires, students of an engaged mindset can select and explore learning objectives designed to stimulate learning inquiry and outcomes measureable against identified course standards in post-secondary education.

Leadership in the Classroom

What underlies servant leadership is the motivation behind the actions of leaders. "Servant-leadership emphasizes increased service to others, a holistic approach to work, building a sense of community, and the sharing of power in decision making" (Spears & Lawrence, 2002, p. 4). Teachers in leadership capacity can be defined by how they use their authority and influence. "At its core, servant-leadership is a long-term, transformational approach to life and work - in essence, a way of being - that has the potential for creating positive change throughout our society" (Spears & Lawrence, 2002, p. 4). Servant leaders are not leaders based on position or leadership role; they lead according to their calling, vision, and principles.

> The servant-leader is servant first. It begins with the natural feeling that one wants to serve, to serve first. Then conscious choice brings one to aspire to lead. The best test is: Do those served grow as persons; do they while being served, become healthier, freer, more autonomous, more likely to themselves to become servants? (Greenleaf, 1970, p. 15)

An effective approach for teachers to empower self-authorized team leaders is the adherence to the seven pillars of leadership character. The seven pillars are values that serve as a foundation for effective self-authorized team leadership. Sipe and Frick (2009) discussed seven pillars of servant leadership as 1) a person of character, 2) who put people first, 3) skilled communicator, 4) compassionate collaborator, 5) has foresight, 6) is a systems thinker, and 7) leads with moral authority. Exemplifying these pillars as guidelines in the classroom encourages respect and the value of diversity, which results in greater learning. Self-authorized team leadership is a concept that places the responsibility of leadership on the shoulders of each team member (Urichuck, 2007). When students assume responsibility for their actions and relationships with others, they share learning responsibilities in all aspects of knowledge dissemination.

Stewardship demands a vision and mission for immediate tasks as well as for the future. "Stewardship is the willingness to be accountable for the well-being of the larger organization by operating in service, rather than in control, of those around us" (Block, 1993, p. 32). Servant-leadership and stewardship come from very similar conceptual themes. Stewardship more generally emphasizes leadership stepping forward and taking ownership of the endeavor by doing the right thing with morally-founded purpose. Servant-leadership, conversely, promotes leading from behind through providing for the group with encouragement, direction, motivation, and resources. The approach combines the stewardship philosophy of Block (2002) and the servant leadership philosophy of Greenleaf (1970), and is termed: *Stewardship-living*. Specifically, *stewardship-living* encourages individuals at all levels of the organization to practice through promotion of individual talents, resources, strengths, and skills comprehensive organizational leadership behaviors dedicated to the mutual productivity of the organization as founded on meeting requirements of unilaterally placed organization stakeholders. Incorporating many of the stewardship principles of Block and the servant-leadership principles of Greenleaf and Sears (2002), stewardship-living goes more deeply and inclusive throughout the organization than does servant leadership, and has greater leadership expectations of all members than does Block's (1993) stewardship.

Lifting up all individuals of the learning environment toward higher potential and active fulfillment of leadership, stewardship-living asks each to commit him or herself to the benefit of all, and rewards the individual with true membership, respect and relationship within and across the association, network, or learning environment. From this understanding, stewardship-living promotes morally and ethically based shared leadership with a set of member-created values and a principle-based foundation of inclusion and relationship amongst stakeholders of the organization.

Learning Theory and Faculty Style

Descartes is known for trying to create a paradigm of knowledge that provides certainty. Philosophers refer to this as normative epistemology, which is a philosophical format that seeks to create norms or criteria, which justifies knowledge. The idea that certain sets of norms are correct and have a special status requires justification. Horner and Westacott (2000) discussed that normative principles might seek justification in the following principles:

1. Belief counts as knowledge if it coheres with an existing network of beliefs.

2. Belief counts as knowledge if it can be deduced from premises that the majority of people would accept as obviously true.

3. Belief counts as knowledge if it entails statements that can be confirmed experimentally. (p. 58)

The term *philosophy* has its origin in ancient Greece and refers to a passion or love for wisdom. Christenson (2001) stated, "philosophy is disciplined critical reflection (about fundamental ideas) that springs from wonder" (p. 4). Wonder is connected to the concept of wisdom (Christenson, 2001). Philosophers such as Plato and Aristotle used the term wonder to help identify responses that bewilder, amaze, puzzle, and sometimes even create shock in our lives. The philosopher uses questions as a tool to uncover basic issues and challenge faulty thinking. Ultimately, the philosopher must ask the radical questions about lives that are often filled with a degree of mystery. Philosophers are life-long learners who are on a journey that requires both persistence and humility. Ultimately, life-long learners have a mental disposition or mindset that empowers them to pursue the challenges associated with critical thinking and sharing ideas through verbal and written communication.

Ideally, all schools should lead individuals from a place of lesser desirability to an area of greater desirability. Training places an emphasis on the *how to* and sharpening specific skills. Education refers to asking the *what and why* questions of life and is end oriented. Education is a more holistic approach to learning that makes people more aware of opportunities, responsibilities, and human potential. As an aspect of holistic education, the basis for learning and teaching is dependent on the method of interaction between the teacher and the learner. This method emphasizes the teacher-learner interaction that extends beyond the use of teaching aids and focuses on the holistic approach. Holistic education is comprised of "five basic components: knowledge, self, personal and professional development, discipline, and learning and teaching" (Batson, 2008, p. 47). The teacher-learner interaction is fundamental to develop learners into critical and independent thinkers (Miller, 2005). The use of the holistic approach could be integral to developing an educational reform system using the theories of Mindset and Differentiated Instruction, a method of teaching that involves matching learning styles with abilities (Sousa & Tomlinson, 2011).

Contemporary definitions of critical thinking usually stress outcomes and mental strategies, but neglect describing basic behavioral characteristics and skills required for critical thinking and knowledge acquisition. Lipman (1991) observed that a more general approach would emphasize good judgment or wisdom because doing so would connect the concepts of knowledge, personal experience, and the quality of choices that are made by the individual. A holistic approach recognizes that all choices are not equally good, which brings a more dynamic dimension to the process of critical thinking. In fact, Lipman (1995) asked, what is wisdom? He answered his own question by observing that wisdom refers to making intelligent or excellent judgments. Therefore, wisdom includes a variety of skills such as problem solving, but is a more general idea. Ultimately, wisdom involves the practical application of knowledge that is built upon a series of good judgments. Wisdom is an educational outcome or product of critical thinking.

Student Mindset and Engagement

A mindset is a fixed mental attitude or disposition that predetermines ones responses or can even become a habit (Preacher, 2008). One reason that adult learning is effective is because the faculty who facilitate the courses are able to integrate real-world experience into the course objectives and students are able to apply learning into personal and career interests. Education is most valuable when classroom or educational learning can bridge the gap between theoretical textbook or classroom learning to real-life application. The power behind faculty that can transfer professional experience, along with scholarly literature knowledge, is unparalleled in an academic setting.

In the classroom, faculty experience and scholarly knowledge can be used to engage and motivate students to master the learning objectives of the course objectives. Understanding that all students learn differently is critical. Through differentiation of course management principles and criteria, facilitators can use this knowledge to implement various learning methods and to create multiple assessments. This approach enables facilitators to meet the needs of students to be mindfully engaged with the course topics and learning objectives while encouraging student success both inside and outside the classroom.

Dweck (2007) developed a distinction in mindsets: fixed, growth-oriented, and productive. What people think and believe about their own intelligence has far-reaching benefits and consequences. For a Fixed-Mind (FM) person, external feedback is very important, validating or invalidating the person. Fixed minded people seek items and experiences that make them feel secure, powerful, and superior. Those with a so-called fixed-mindset see intelligence as unchangeable and develop a tendency to focus on proving that they have that characteristic instead of focusing on the process of learning (Dweck, 2007). FMs tend to avoid difficult challenges because failing on these could cause them to lose their intelligent appearance. This disregard of challenge and learning hinders them in the development of their learning and in their performance. The fixed-mindset can hinder a student in developing knowledge, skills, and abilities (Dweck, 2007).

For a Growth-Minded (GM) person, the feeling regarding one's effort is most that matters; the result is less important than the effort. Growth-minded people seek challenges, where they feel uncertain about the outcome and risk failing because of the learning the experience could provide. GMs welcome questioning, criticism, and can separate the bad experiences from their value as individuals. A Productive Mindset (PM) makes the best use of resources - time, energy, and efforts and making the most and best of what of a situation while enjoying the process. To make the most of who we are and what we have, there are certain qualities or characteristics that assist us in accomplishing that end, such as curiosity, desire or motivation, vision, critical thinking, self-confidence, persistence, positive attitude or outlook, open-mindedness, and balance. Faculty in the classroom, through the enactment of stewardship and servant leadership, can strategically design education practices to better encourage more productive learning-capable mindsets for students by facilitating the classroom experience to provide differentiated learning experiences and gainful outcomes for all.

As differentiation becomes a new way of thinking about the classroom, the processes in which students were taught is no longer effective (Daggett, Butts, & Smith, 2002). A new way of looking at post-secondary education must be adopted to accommodate the different levels of mindsets of students. Fortunately, productive and growth mindsets can be taught. People who have learned to develop a growth mindset know that effort is the main key to creating knowledge and skills (Dweck, 2007). Developing a growth mindset in adults would be advantageous in the classroom and achieve more significant learning outcomes for students.

Differentiation Instruction

Differentiation of instruction is a student-centered approach to teaching that recognizes the varied and diverse nature of learners, including the way they learn, and providing students with different avenues for acquiring content and processing ideas, to develop teaching materials so that all students within a classroom can learn effectively, regardless of differences in ability (Allan & Tomlinson, 2000). Differentiation teaching encourages synergy and innovation. Differentiated Instruction is critical in today's learning environment because it enables teachers to open up learning opportunities for all students by offering varied learning experiences, allowing teachers to put research-based best practices into a meaningful context for learning. Teachers using differentiated instruction understand and use the assessment as a critical tool to drive instruction and add new instructional strategies to teachers' "toolboxes"—introducing or reinforcing techniques to help teachers focus on essentials of curriculum. Giving administrators, teachers, and students an instructional management system to more efficiently meet the demands of high stakes testing, differentiation teaching also meets curriculum requirements in a meaningful way for achieving students' success (Staff Development for Educators, Inc., 2006).

Clapper (2002) performed a quantitative, quasi-experimental study and explored the differences and effect of leadership instruction delivered through direct and differentiated means of instruction. The study used a pre-test and post-test that were administered to a convenience-sampling at one of the largest, and most successful inner-city U.S. Army JROTC (Junior Reserve Officers Training Corps (JROTC) programs. One control group and one experimental group received an assessment about identifying the leadership principles in action after the participants viewed short video clips. While both the control and experimental groups achieved statistically significance differences between the pretest and posttest, the experimental group that received differentiated instruction "achieved a statistically significant effect size and scored higher than the control group on each test" (Clapper, 2002, p. 78). Clapper's study showed the importance that a search for possibilities could do to increase student achievement and personal growth that could be achieved by differentiating the instruction.

Differentiation of instruction responds to a student's learner profile with respect to learning objective identification and assessment identification and demonstration. Teachers can differentiate content, learning process, and product assessment criteria and strategies according to student readiness, interests, and learning profile (Sousa & Tomlinson, 2011). Content includes both what the teacher plans for the students to learn and how the student gains access to desired information, understanding, and skills. Assessment products refer to the items a student can use to demonstrate what he or she understands and can be able to do because of an extended period of study (Sousa & Tomlinson, 2011). Differentiation of course materials contain student assessment criteria to gain student interest, curious, engagement, and passion for learning. The customization of course materials uses standardized university curriculum models (Sousa & Tomlinson, 2011).

Customizing assignments would mean providing alternatives for faculty and students to explore options of learning objective exploration and engagement, along with assessment criteria to demonstrate achievement of stated objectives. How students learn and faculty facilitate can include creativity, engagement, reflection, and insight. Using approaches beyond questions and answers, and beyond textbooks and lectures, can refresh a facilitator and engage the students (Sousa & Tomlinson, 2011).

Student characteristics can include:

a. Readiness: Levels of difficulty, varied groups, scaffolding of activities by adding or removing mentors/mentees, modeling, demonstration, or manipulative

b. Interest: Providing choices, resource discovery, mentors and peers with shared interests, material access

c. Learning Profile: learning styles, student talents, intelligence/knowledge profiles. (Sousa & Tomlinson, 2011)

Teachers seeking a way to promote cooperation, collaboration, and task completion should consider profiling students' readiness and interests.

Objectives, materials, and assessment customization would include faculty compiling a list of course topics, content, and key words based on the course objectives and providing this list to students. Each student could then choose from the list based on his or her personal and career interests, one or two for each week or three or four to cover several weeks of the course that they wanted to investigate. The expectation would be that students would research and select appropriate videos, podcasts, business journals, peer reviewed articles, databases, and other multimedia, plus scholarly text chapters, to support their objectives and topics using the sources provided. To demonstrate learning objective achievement, students would be expected to create an illustration or scenario describing an organization issue, problem to be resolved, decision-making scenario, or diagram of strategic activity. Many university libraries include excellent data on many organization students can use for these scenarios. Students could also use an organization that they are personally familiar with for examples. With practice in library and literature review research activities, students should become proficient with obtaining necessary information, and hopefully, their curiosity will spur them forward. Library resources could include relevant databases, such as Country Watch, Direction of Trade Statistics, EIU Country Data, Euromonitor International, and Culturegrams (Sousa & Tomlinson, 2011).

Assessment example: For Week 1 student activities could include selecting personal learning objectives and topics from a list of course topic-relevant learning objectives provided by the university and supplemented by the faculty based on his or her professional expertise and an understanding of student interests and experiences. A proposal by the student would explain the student's work plan and timeline needed for each topic chosen as well as the materials involved. Additionally, each student's plan could contain metrics for assessment fulfillment achievement for demonstration of learning objectives. Student fulfillment of the learning objectives and assessment criteria could include various media such as papers, videos, role-plays, and presentations. In all assessment documentation, the validity of information presented should be supported by sources of authority with cross-validation between sources (Sousa & Tomlinson, 2011).

Summary Supporting Research

Imagine an adult learning environment in which faculty can impact the learner mindset through an effective practice of stewardship, with a vision of engaging students in differentiated learning, designed to maximize engagement with the learning process and student belief in their capacity to achieve high academic and knowledge-demonstration outcomes. Capturing the interest and passion of the student to achieve and demonstrate learning goals and outcomes should be the priority and mission of every classroom. Through a combined practice of servant and stewardship leadership practices, faculty can begin to set the stage upon which learning theory choreographed with student initiative and differentiated curriculum can make possible, significant student outcomes. In an environment modified and supplemented toward student learning desires, students of an engaged mindset can select and explore learning objectives designed to stimulate learning inquiry and outcomes measureable against identified course standards in post-secondary education. The application of learning objectives toward personally selected interests allows more significant engagement, which can be applied directly to that which is relevant and most meaningful for the student in post-secondary education.

REFERENCES

Allan, S. D., & Tomlinson, C. A. (2000). *Leadership for differentiating schools and classrooms.* Alexandria, VA: Association for Supervision and Curriculum Development.

Batson, G. (2008). *Head start and at-risk students' perceptions of administrators, practitioners, and parents.* (Doctoral dissertation). Retrieved from ProQuest Theses and Dissertations database. (UMI No. 3323351).

Block, P. (1993). *Stewardship: Choosing service over self-interest.* San Francisco, CA: Berrett-Koehler Publishers.

Christenson, T. (2001). *Wonder and critical reflection: An invitation to philosophy.* Upper Saddle Creek, NJ: Prentice-Hall.

Clapper, T. (2011). *The effect of differentiated instruction on JROTC leadership training.* Capella University.

Daggett, L., Butts, J., & Smith, K. (2002). The development of an organizing framework to implement AACN guidelines for nursing education. *Journal of Nursing Education, 41*(1), 34–37.

Dweck, C. (2007). *Mindset: The new psychology of success.* New York, NY: Ballantine Books.

Greenleaf, R. (1970). *The servant leader.* Mahwah, NJ: Paulist Press.

Greenleaf, R., & Sears, L (2002). *Servant leadership: A journey into the nature of legitimate power.* Mahwah, NJ: Paulist Press.

Horner, C., & Westacott, E. (2000). *Thinking through philosophy: An introduction.* Cambridge, UK: Cambridge University Press.

Lipman, M. (1991). *Thinking in education.* New York, NY: Cambridge University Press.

Lipman, M. (1995). Critical thinking—what can it be? In A. L. Ornstein & L. S. Behar (Eds.), *Contemporary Issues in Curriculum* (pp. 145–152). Boston, MA: Allyn & Bacon.

Miller, R. (2005). *Holistic education encyclopedia of informal education.* Retrieved from http://www.infed.org/biblio/holisticeducation.htm

Preacher, S. (2008). *What is a mindset?* Retrieved from http://www.simonpreacher.com/blog/success_journal/what-is-a-mindset/

Sipe, J., & Frick, D. (2009) *Seven pillars of leadership: Practicing the wisdom of leading by serving.* Mahwah, NJ: Paulist Press.

Sousa, D. A., & Tomlinson, C. A. (2011). *Differentiation and the brain: How neuroscience supports the learner-friendly classroom.* Bloomington, IN: Solution Tree Press.

Spears, L. C., & Lawrence, M. (Eds.), (2002). *Focus on leadership: Servant leadership for the twenty-first century.* New York, NY: John Wiley and Sons.

Staff Development for Educators, Inc. (2006). *Differentiated instruction.* Retrieved from http://www.differentiatedinstruction.com/

Urichuck, B. (2007). *Disciplines to inspire a results-oriented team: The seven pillars of leadership character.* Retrieved from http://www.bobu .com/newsletter/july07/pillars.pdf

About the Authors

Southern California author Dr. Judy Fisher-Blando holds the following accredited degrees: a Bachelor of Science (BS) in Business Management; a Master's of Art (MA) in Organizational Management; and a Doctorate of Management (DM) in Organizational Leadership from the University of Phoenix School of Advanced Studies. She has also obtained her Six Sigma Black Belt certificate.

Dr. Judy an adjunct professor for Walden University and University of Phoenix, teaching classes in organizational behavior and research methodologies.

She is an expert on Workplace Bullying, having written her research dissertation on *Workplace Bullying: Aggressive Behavior and Its Effect on Job Satisfaction and Productivity.* In addition, she is a Life Coach, coaching leaders on how to develop High Performance Organizations, coaching the targets of workplace bullies, and giving presentations on Finding and Measuring your Joy.

To reach Dr. Judy Fisher-Blando for information on any of these topics, and for executive coaching or coaching on workplace bullying, please e-mail judyblando@gmail.com

Dr. Denise L. Land holds the following accredited degrees, including a Bachelor of Science (BS) in Gerontology and Masters of Social Work from California State University, Sacramento; and a Doctorate of Management (DM) in Organizational Leadership from the University of Phoenix School of Advanced Studies.

Dr. D., as she is known to her students, is a university professor on faculty with Walden University, where she also serves on several doctoral committees and is a faculty mentor. Faculty teaching activities include strategic planning, leadership, and research methods. In addition to her faculty work with Walden, she also has university faculty experience in the areas of human services, psychology, communications, research, management, leadership, and critical thinking.

Additional published works include her dissertation: *Identifying Strategic Leadership Practice Motivators of Nonprofit Employee Retention;* and "Socio-Technical Systems Advancement: Making Distance Learning Changes That Count" *Journal of U.S. Distance Learning Association.*

To reach Dr. Denise Land for information on any of these topics, please e-mail her: dlland@ftcnet.net

CHAPTER 3

Teachers as Mentors

Dr. Rene Contreras

According to the National Center for Education Statistics (2010), 1992 was the baseline year used to measure secondary student academic performance in the traditional academic disciplines. What was once considered the traditional curriculum, since 1992, traditional subjects such as: reading, mathematics, and science have been de-emphasized. Many organizations such as the National Council of Teachers of Mathematics (NCTM) and similar organizations are against the use of student graduation examinations also known as high-stakes tests ("Wikipedia," 2011). The research data gathered within the last two decades reflect a decline in student test scores that have declined ("U.S. Department of Education," 2007–2008). Béland and Vergniolle de Chantal (2004) noted that starting in 1993, the Clinton Administration created a new social welfare state and a new social policy paradigm that evolved within the America's education culture.

Béland and Vergniolle de Chantal (2004) stressed that after the early 2000s, historical institutionalism had contributed to the political and sociological analysis of public policy, especially in the area of welfare state politics and the post-secondary system. The social welfare state occurred although voters approved billions in new monies that went into the education social welfare state. Despite the shift in public policy and the increase in funding for education, public education has not improved as measured by graduation rates, and student test scores ("U.S. Department of Education," 2007–2008). In addition to federal tax dollars, voters approved tax dollars from state lotteries, state income tax increases, state sales tax increases, property tax increases, and other forms of tax increases targeted to improve America's faltering education throughout America. Politician's emphasis has been in retaining or funding teachers and not retaining quality teachers.

Since the early 2000s, the United States Federal Government levied new social programs in the name of multicultural academics regarding secondary schools curricula. During 1992–2008, student scores declined and as parents asked for more from educators for their children, politicians at all levels of government promised quick fixes to a complex social welfare state. In the end, the billions of tax dollars went to finance school buildings, upgrade school and classroom computers, increase teachers' salaries through collective bargaining in 53.5% of United States school districts, transforming America's teacher's union one of the nation's largest and most powerful unions ("U.S. Department of Education," 2007–2008).

Since 1992, school districts retained outdated academic curricula's and outdated textbooks. Only ten states had a textbook selection standard that was used in recommending the curriculum and textbooks used by their districts, and of these states, only six selected the textbooks used within its states in an effort to promote standardized programs. During 2000–2006, of the 50 United States that considered curriculum development in their annual budgets, Louisiana, Minnesota, Vermont, New Mexico, Oklahoma, and Tennessee selected new textbooks in an effort to update their curricula's ("U.S. Department of Education," 2007–2008). By understanding the factors that changed what was once known as the world's best education system, one can understand how a simple theory like mentoring, which has been always a crucial aspect of teaching continues to serve as the most important role in America's education system. Secondary educators must understand mentoring theory and how students benefit from the mentoring relationship.

This section is not a study of the United States education system. Instead, the goal of this chapter will offer a possible solution, mentoring, to help postsecondary education students achieve academic success. Students agree that early in their school years that they had teachers who influenced them. By offering an alternate solution to society, mentoring of secondary students by educators indirectly provides the modern organization. Potential benefits that help develop the teacher-student mentorship relationship and contributes to developing student leadership were examined.

Mentorship and Education System Background

Two factors important to examine are: a) what helps develop the teacher-student mentor relationship; and, b) what contributes to developing student leaders. It is important to understand the American political culture that influence the education system starting with two key pieces of legislation enacted during the Clinton presidency: the 'Unfunded Mandates Reform Act', and the 'Personal Responsibility and Work Opportunity Reconciliation Act Eight' (Béland & Vergniolle de Chantal, 2004). These two pieces of legislation launched the American welfare state, but few comprehensive and theoretically informed studies have been published to study or properly measure the institutional and ideological effects of social policy (Béland & Vergniolle de Chantal).

Thomas and Van Derhaar (2005) noted that as teachers typically deal with issues of diversity and racism in classroom settings, education, and multicultural curricula are linked to the idea that education institutions can shape policy changes between federalism reform and welfare state development (Béland & Hacker, 2004; Lieberman, 2002). The policy change introduced by the higher education institutions highlight the importance of teacher responsibilities for mentoring of students in school (Capel, 2011). At the same time, the United States Federal Government spent billions of dollars in what the Federal Government classified as future human capital investment (Elementary and Secondary Education Act, 2009).

Béland and Vergniolle de Chantal (2004) posited that the concepts of 'unfunded mandate' and 'block grant' embodied in the new legislation enacted during the Clinton presidency are key elements of a gradual reshaping of social policy and intergovernmental relations in America. Despite the radical character of the conservative ideological crusade, the United States welfare state is still generally characterized by an intimate link between centralization rooted in a well-established ideological and the comprehensive social policies (Béland & Vergniolle de Chantal, 2004). Understanding the social change that these laws had on the American education culture helps one understand how difficult the social change influence students and educators working within the complex education environment and the impact on the mentorship relationship.

An important factor for society to understand is that teachers not only serve as subject-matter experts, but also are responsible for serving as mentors. Becoming an educator consists of a collaborative mindset that "begins with teacher candidates acting as observers and participants in both the general and special education systems" (Fullerton, Ruben, McBride, & Bert, 2011, p. 33). Society needs new teachers to execute the United States collective vision and establish the latest teaching curricula levied by the education leaders and the government jointly, which requires an educational-based ideology.

Dunleavy (2004) posited that the use of a mentor will help individuals "develop organizational skills" (p. 30). A crucial aspect omitted by the United States legislators is the omission of education experts during social welfare debates that replace policy maker's views or opinions with "political and technical choices through frames that legitimize under the premise of need for reform" (Béland & Vergniolle de Chantal, 2004, p. 243). That provides the voice and point of view of educators to the political system, which is not influenced by Special Interest Groups. Instead, United States legislators listen to one of 174 Special Interest Groups that each gives legislators incentives to support the SIGs interests (Ulanoff, 2011), and not the interests of their constituents or the general education community. The education community is interested in school curricula that includes mentoring theories, which ultimately results in student career development.

According to Fullerton, Ruben, McBride, and Bert (2011), traditional secondary educators' curriculum no longer covers the basic courses formerly taught during the 1970s or prior that included reading, mathematics, home economics or science, English, American history, physical education, and many elective courses. For example, unlike the traditional academics settings taught since 1992, some states changed their academic curricula to include what has been renamed as social education course curriculum. Fullerton et al. (2011) suggested that the learning community (faculty, teacher candidates, mentor teachers, student teachers, and supervisors) is experiencing the following topics in college in an effort to help him or her become better prepared in today's classroom:

> (1) Adolescent Learners in Inclusive Settings; (2) Adolescents with Learning Differences; (3) Multicultural and Urban Education; (4) Inclusive Classrooms; (5) Collaborative Teaming and the Special Education Process; (6) Advocacy and Transition Planning; (7) Classroom-Based Assessment; (8) Instructional Methods: Literacy Instruction; (9) Diagnostic Assessment, and (10) Math and Content Area Instruction. (p. 3)

Within the new education environment of limited special education classrooms, educators were limited in their abilities to identify students with learning disabilities. This change resulted in a noted decline in national standardized test scores administration of a merged secondary and special education program during the new welfare state (Fullerton et al., 2011). Even though mentors provide students specific improvement target areas and academic support to students.

Fullerton, Ruben, McBride, and Bert (2011) argued that a more serious national issue in the social cultural change was in the administration of the deemphasized traditional academic curricula. The current Secondary Dual Educator's Program (SDEP) research did not use the educational organizational culture as an investigation objective but examined the effects of mentor training programs used and the effects of student achievement (Fullerton et al., 2011, pp. 32–33). Fullerton et al. stressed that understanding of the benefits of mentor training programs and the influence on student achievement benefited special education student teachers. It set the stage for secondary and special education candidates to collaborate initially as content area teachers (Fullerton et al., 2011).

Mentoring Benefits: Teacher-Students Relationship

The post-secondary education mentoring practices and their influence on the secondary organizational environment were examined searching for mentor patterns and the role of teachers in developing secondary school students who may benefit society. Bennis (2004) noted that leadership is a blend of personal behaviors that allows industries to recruit employees who become the organization's dedicated leaders during the development process. Teacher development includes a full range of academic, ability, race, class, culture, and linguistic diversity among adolescent learners but lacks mentoring theories (Fullerton et al., 2011). Contreras' (2008) research offered 72 mentoring theories to assist organizations in developing employees or students as part of the unit's career development effort.

The mentorship association ultimately contributes to student achievement whether the mentor contribution is positive or negative. The teaching culture is compared to political theories and leadership development is associated to political constituencies. Various political theorists from Plato to Mao have expressed various positions on the essentials of leadership (Bass, 1990). The literature on mentorship provided an appropriate correspondence between the perceived needs of student development and the realistic means of the mentorship relationship. Many factors within the secondary education culture influence the mentor relationship.

Recent studies have described mentor training programs and the outgrowth of mentorship relationships that vary little by industry (Eby & Allen, 2001). Regardless of the industry, training students to serve as future leaders is a primary goal of organizations whose goal is to teach students: leadership, responsible citizenship, and service to community, life-coping skills, physical fitness, health, hygiene, job skills, and academic excellence ("Institute of Education Services, 2010). "Although many organizations have created extensive recruiting and retention programs, most industries have not filled the required leadership positions due to limited qualified employees" (Contreras, 2008, p. 17).

According to Jones and Straker (2006), the issue of mentor training consistency and equality is a variable that raises the need for quality training within initial teacher training (Foster, 2000, 2001). Understanding the teacher-student mentorship role may help organizations understand the mentorship culture, especially as educators are expected to deal with a varied student base. Language deficiencies and organizational culture differences must be clearly understood by educators. Then the education environment can take advantage of an effective mentoring program and organizations may contribute to attracting and retaining quality teachers. Mentors should act as assessors or gatekeepers by balancing students with the other "demands made upon themselves as practicing teachers" (Jones & Straker, 2006, p. 166).

Eby and Allen (2004) suggested that an important issue discussed by mentoring pupils includes mentoring practices that are associated with career growth, jobs, and career satisfaction. Earlier mentoring theory implied that if organizations guided individuals successfully through systematic mentoring programs, they would develop personally and professionally throughout the learner's career development. Gibson and Jefferson (2006) asserted that family, peers, community groups, and the student's mentor influence the mentorship relationship. It is important that a teacher be personally committed in promoting the student's career development as part of the teacher-student mentor relationship. Current mentoring literature suggests the mentoring partnership is developed over time that may experience several changes in self-concepts and social relationships (Gibson & Jefferson, 2006). Jones and Straker (2006) noted that research literature generated during the past 15 years suggests that positive relationships with teachers and his or her mentee enhance career development.

Today's Education Bureaucratic Organization

The problem under investigation is the lack of knowledge of the benefits of teachers as mentors. According to Capel (2011), test results "showed that only 17% of subject mentors perceived that they had major responsibility for supporting students" (p. 13). Although mentoring and coaching theories are part of the educators training curriculum, such training is limited. This deficiency exists even though educators play an important role in society. Even within the education system itself, further investigation is needed to determine the relationship between the responsibilities that mentors have in supporting students. Another area requiring further study is the benefits students receive from teachers serving as mentors.

Drucker (1974) asserted that a lifetime continual training is the correct approach for self-improvement. Leadership training programs fail because: a) powerful leaders withhold support, b) the training results are improperly measured, and c) leadership training is not aligned with company goals and vision (Ready & Conger, 2003). The United States Federal Government asserted itself in fiscal year 2010 when the Congress appropriated $14.5 billion for Title I, Part A of the Elementary and Secondary Education Act of 1965 (ESEA), which funds services to students in schools with high concentrations of students from low-income families (Elementary and Secondary

Education Act, 2009). Although the secondary education culture uses a global work environment, application of traditional leadership theories are not different to civilian organizations. Unless education leaders support mentor training programs, the teacher-student mentor program will not succeed.

According to the "National Council on Teacher Quality" (2011), 200,000 teacher candidates enter the education system each year. Of these teachers, institutions lack a clear and rigorous criteria for the selection of cooperating teachers for selection as mentors ("National Council on Teaching Quality," 2011). "Nearly two out of three institutions fail to assess the mentoring capacity of a teacher or at least to require any mentoring training" ("National Council on Teaching Quality," 2011, p. 2). Education institutions agree that the placement process and the selection of exemplary cooperating teachers through an effective mentoring program help place only those teachers in the top quartile of performance, as assessed by their school principals, and institutions ("National Council on Teaching Quality," 2011).

Gibson and Jefferson (2006) contended that current academic literature suggests an important mentoring issue includes forming identity that is a combination of the constructs of self-concept and self-esteem often defined as primary development tasks. A practical implication of mentoring practices within a secondary educational organization, which encourages mentor self-awareness as an understanding that student's career development may occur because of the mentorship relationship. According to Eby et al. (2004), mentoring theory may provide some reporting differences on how the mentor and student commence or maintain the mentorship relationship. Educators have the potential of changing the general attitudes of their students who benefit society (Juodeikaite & Leliugiene, 2009). Mentoring relationships has notable potential for improving organizational performance and successful organizations.

Béland and Vergniolle de Chantal contended (2004) that an opponent of bureaucratic 'big government' was President Reagan who supported deregulation and a period that the American education system prospered. The secondary education bureaucratic organization limits the teacher-student mentor development due to ideology factors similar to command-and-control structure. The research literature analysis revealed that within the education system, due to factors such as compliance regulations, the mentorship relationship limited the amount that a student could achieve from the teacher-student mentoring relationship. According to Béland and Vergniolle de Chantal, Washington playing an unprecedented regulatory role in the United States, has added compliance regulations to limit the teacher's ability to freely develop the teacher-student mentorship relationship.

Mentoring by Educators

Spears and Lawrence (2002) stressed that "we are beginning to see that traditional, autocratic, and hierarchical modes of leadership are yielding to a newer model—one based on teamwork" (p. 2). Technology changes since the 1990s have changed student's expectations for increased and better quality of personal communications and supervisor feedback common in effective mentoring relationships. An important factor about effective leadership training is recognizing different learning styles of learners. Educators agree that education allows students to develop within their community and country, and allows nations to compete and survive in the global economy (Hamzah, 2010).

Kaye and Jordan-Evans (2003) suggested that employees expect their work efforts rewarded on behalf of the organization. Because mentoring theory is part of the leadership theory curriculum, understanding the relationship associated between student learning styles and mentorship partnerships are important. The role of the mentor with the mentorship relationship is important to a successful partnership. Within the study of mentoring theory, the charismatic mentor is more successful with the mentoring process. "Psychoanalytic theories have been used to interpret how the interaction of the personalities of leaders and situations is dramatized in times of crisis" (Contreras, 2008, p. 36). To associate the mentor as a leader helps attain student benefits and enhance the student's performance.

Spears and Lawrence (2002) cited Williams (2002) who mentioned that multiple studies reflect that "of the many styles of leadership that researchers have documented—bureaucratic, charismatic, democratic, intellectual, executive, patrimonial, and representative" (p. 67) a rarer type of discernible or consistent pattern of leadership traits has yet to be found. Williams notes that as part of the leadership task, the leader never knows for sure what the results will be because leaders cannot predict whether others will benefit (Spears & Lawrence, 2002). Contreras (2008) posited that both positive and negative elements of charismatic leadership have been explored. A growing recognition exists suggesting that formal mentoring programs allow individuals to be successful throughout their careers (Haines, 2003).

For example, according to The United States Department of Education, recent school district surveys reflect that districts are looking to hire new teachers from the business industry that may offer new leadership insights for its students ("U.S. Department of Education," 2007–2008). The U.S. Federal Government offers programs such as the Economic Opportunity Act of 1964 (Public Law 88–452) authorized grants for college work-study programs for students from low-income families (Elementary and Secondary Education Act, 2009). The military has a similar Troops to Teachers program where military members can receive a teaching college degree paid by the Federal Government in exchange for teaching 5 years in a low-income school district ("Troops to Teachers," 2011).

Mentoring activities are self-perpetuating and formal mentoring programs provide the mentorship relationship boundaries (Haines, 2003). The change in student satisfaction needs by young professionals is becoming an important educators' and organizations' challenge. An important factor to any successful mentorship relationship puts growth of the individual first within the mentorship relationship (Dunleavy, 2004). A mentorship relationship requires the student have a clearly defined set of professional development goals based on organizational needs. Mentoring partnerships could prove to be effective training tools that influence student achievement that indirectly benefit the organizational culture (Herzberg, 2003).

Mentoring Training and Theory

Gaskin, Lumpkin, and Tenant (2003) asserted that research studies have found that mentoring research has detected job satisfaction for the student because of the mentoring partnership of students with mentors were more satisfied with their jobs. Factors influencing student achievement were examined that were established through organizational effort. The student or mentee academic achievement component examined in the preceding sections offer an appreciation of the sources of student professional goals. Mentoring pupils suggested that to consider a mentorship training program successful, the mentor program must have some measurement.

Jackson's (2005) study mentioned, "Training gives comprehensive and extensive examination of key aspects to leadership and a key component is that all participants have a mentor" (p. 74). The mentoring effects examined in the preceding sections offer an appreciation of the sources of students' expectations because of the mentorship relationship. Many theories pertaining to the characteristics of the mentor relationship influence student achievement. Differences of opinion exist relating to the grade or position of each group member within the organization participating in the training process (Jackson, 2005). According to Ambrose (2003), the first step to building a mentor and protégé mentoring relationship requires becoming acquainted with each other.

Capel (2011) noted that although preparing students is not the responsibility of any specific school staff, the major responsibility falls on teachers serving as professional mentors as perceived by students. Research suggests education and civilian organizations focus on motivating and engaging employees in classroom and work environments (Ledbetter, 2003). Mentoring studies seem to incorporate three multifaceted essential considerations: (1) the personality, motivational, or behavioral traits of the leader; (2) the nature of the followers or group, and (3) the problem, situation, or organizational context involved (Bass, 1990; Collins, 2001; Equizabal, 2004). Within the educational experience, students are more successful if a teacher acts in a mentoring capacity than simply as a teacher ("National Council on Teaching Quality," 2011).

Cooper and Pagotto (2003) posited that as corporate funds used for leadership development and technology training become insufficient, organizations must use these limited funds wisely. Several authors have addressed the changing demands of leadership in various settings (Wren, 1995). Each work setting and organizational culture has a different impact on the student and mentor because company rules are part of unit goals and visions. Classroom and leadership training that includes mentoring theories contributes to student achievement, benefits the mentorship partnership development, and enhances work accomplishments. The school-based training and channeled communications learned from the school experience help students develop competencies that become useful later in the workplace (Capel, 2011).

Garvey and Alred (2003) advocated "analyses of mentoring through the application of different theoretical views, covering psychological, interpersonal, sociological, and political aspects" (p. 8). The mentorship relationship is most beneficial when the social resources connect with the protégé (Garvey & Alred, 2003). Global strategic thinking is the most important quality that executives look for when identifying future leaders (Wire, 2003). Programs centered on developing leadership skills expose students to different leadership theories (King & Anderson, 2004). The student attains the possible long-term benefits within the mentorship relationship.

Mentoring Achievement and Benefits

Armstrong, Allinson, and Hayes (2002) suggested, "The effects of the mentoring relationship and its influence on protégé achievement seem to be centered more on the functions the mentor performs" (p. 2). The mentoring partnership develops a relationship between mentor training and student achievement. Armstrong et al. indicated that although mentors might benefit from organizational recognition and mentorship relationship benefits, the mentorship problem is complex. Dunleavy (2004) posits the presence of a mentoring partnership can be a key ingredient in job satisfaction and protégé achievement. Supporting students to reach the standard of professional requirements as a major responsibility of teachers serving as mentors included maintaining records of achievement (Capel, 2011). Student achievement should be maximized during the early stages of professional growth because of the teacher-student relationship (Contreras, 2008).

Stokes (2003) noted that damaging consequences for the mentor and student relationship might develop. The mentor might unconsciously ignore the views of the student. The mentor and student should reassess his or her mentorship relationship and make mutually agreed upon changes. Adjustments to the mentoring process require the mentor and student to communicate his or her thoughts to develop the mentorship relationship. For example, 24% of the researched teacher mentors did not perceive him or herself as having a responsibility to his or her students (Capel, 2011).

According to Bass (1990), social learning theories explain the leader-follower relationship because of the leader interaction with the followers, as well with the circumstances involved. Such relationships have become an intricate aspect of theories that fall under this category such as the leader-role theory and the contingency theory. According to Garvey and Alred (2000), although those teaching mentoring reflected 56% interest in teaching mentoring, their research data was "difficult to assess the content of mentor education from this survey" (p. 118). Garvey and Alred suggested that this data sample does not measure whether mentor education is on the increase or not because the current research data was limited.

Bass (1990) suggested that what happens may be explained

by the leader's role, reinforcement of change, and paths to goals. Having examined the various mentor-student factors that apply to the mentor, the student, and the organization, Contreras (2008) considered an overview of the implications of the mentorship relationship. Although the organization and the mentor benefit from a mentoring program, the primary goal should be to increase student performance.

Because not all teachers have the capacity to be mentors, based on performance of their students, quality teachers are becoming mentors ("National Council on Teaching Quality," 2011). Once teachers serving as mentors know the student's needs, teachers have a better understanding of the student's benefits requirements that the mentoring relationship should provide; mainly because the teacher-mentor is committed to an individual student and the mentorship relationship versus the teacher being committed to the entire classroom full of students.

Implications: Teacher / Student Relationship

This section examines mentoring data that explore any empirical information about mentoring benefits. Leaders range from 'all to none' in their effects on their followers (Bass, 1990). Contreras' (2008) research found 72 theorists who suggested the mentoring relationship "develops from the socializing process enhances mentoring opportunities" (see Appendix G). The benefits include students as followers becoming better and more fully informed as they learn to develop their expectations and their satisfaction with their roles that mentors grow.

Contreras (2008) suggested that the foundation for the review of leadership practices develop because of an effective mentorship relationship. The mentor goal is to help the student obtain promotional opportunities. In the mentoring relationship, teachers serving as mentors assist mentees because of their experience, organizational position, and organizational influence.

Bass (1990) indicated that leadership is one of the world's oldest preoccupations. Through the generations, purposeful stories have been told about leaders' competencies, ambitions, shortcomings, duties, rights or privileges, and obligations (Bass, 1990). The preceding sections offer an appreciation of the sources of how the student mentor and the student-teacher mentoring relationships both enhance student achievement. Kaye and Jordan-Evans (2003) asserted that training modern leaders is by nature a continuous process throughout an employee career. Contreras (2008) suggested that depending on the type of organization, the student mentor relationship or the student teacher relationship both benefit from mentoring relationships as long as the organization has an effective training program.

Jones and Straker (2006) suggested that within the mentorship relationship, the difference is that the one-to-one mentoring relationship is uncomfortable to some people. Others like the teacher see his or her interpersonal skills in the classroom as no problem because teachers serve as the class leader (Jones & Straker, 2006). Meanwhile, a committed mentor teacher empowers students through the mentorship relationship because he or she provides specialized guidance and feedback to the student-mentee ("National Council on Teaching Quality," 2011).

Zachary (2000) suggested "Learning is the fundamental process and the primary reason of mentorship" (p. 1). Not promoting independent student development is causing conflict in the mentor relationship by being too ridged (Jones & Straker, 2006). In the mentoring relationship, the key factor may be the mentoring partnership itself and no other factors such as training and individual goals. Mentoring training is the one variable that allows the organization to provide some control within the mentorship relationship that fits the organization's business needs. Formal and informal leadership includes mentoring training programs that provide organizations with opportunities to train their future leaders.

This section examined mentoring benefits and implications. Jones and Straker (2006) posited that some good teachers can be too rigid in their approach and think that their way is the right way, or the only way of doing things. Mentoring is a personal and professional relation, in which the mentorship relationship benefits both the protégé and mentor (Farrell, Digioia, Broderick, & Coates, 2004). Farrell et al. (2004) contended that aspects of modern institutions benefit from mentoring relationships. Like society, teaching institutions continue to search for leadership development methods that provide the leaders of tomorrow.

Conclusion

Collins (2001) argued that within an organizational culture, leaders must explore potential barriers to change and outline strategies for successfully obtaining people from where they are to where they need to be. Leadership is not about style, but about ideas. Jacobson, Rubin, and Selden (2002) suggested a well-designed training program contributes to an organization's performance. Large organizations just like secondary schools confront the same problem in determining which training programs assist them to train or create future leaders (Jacobson, Rubin, & Selden, 2002). Although mentoring training like other industries has not been given any emphasis, perhaps the education environment should consider emphasizing mentoring training mainly because of the student-teacher role that exists within the education culture.

Jacobson et al. (2002) stated that a well-designed training program contributes to an organization's performance by making sure employees have the knowledge and skills needed in current and future jobs. As the mentor develops the mentorship relationship and takes full responsibility for the protégé's learning that normally leads to performance advancements, protégé performance indirectly benefits the organization and its organizational culture. So the creation of a mentor relationship is more conducive to higher student performance whether the relationship is in the academic or business setting.

Jacelon and O'Dell (2005) contended social skills might enhance a protégé's analytical skills to enhance personal and professional achievement. The education environment must understand that educators serving as mentors have an opportunity to mold students as future leaders. The relationship that develops from the socializing process enhances mentoring opportunities. While coaching theories may create productive employees, mentoring theories develop future leaders because of the benefits the mentoring partnership provides to the mentor, the student, and the organization. Although coaches help a protégé develop a skill or set of skills, a teacher serving as a mentor is satisfied with developing a protégé's social and analytical skills that assist a student achieve personal and professional achievement. Education leaders must understand the differences between coaching and mentoring theories.

Collins (2001) suggested that good-to-great companies normally have employees who stay in the company for a long time or quickly leave the company. Senior employees with titles that include chief executive officer, task manager, or supervisor must understand that without having followers they do not meet the requirements of the basic leadership concept that initially starts with educators, which care for their students. This mentoring environment develops the best managers for a specific industry that according to some education experts starts during a student's formal secondary education. This mentoring environment also retains few leaders they need without realizing the reasons. Mentorship studies require further investigation to reveal why organizations have the best managers when instead they need the best leaders.

REFERENCES

Aldisert, L. (2001, April). The value of mentoring. *Bank Marketing, 33*(3), 36–40.

Ambrose, L. (2003). *Mentor's companion* (6th ed.). Chicago, IL: Perrone-Ambrose Associates.

Armstrong, S. J., Allinson, C. W., & Hayes, J. (2002, December). Formal mentoring systems: An examination of the effects of mentor/protégé cognitive styles on the mentoring process. *Journal of Management Studies, 39*(8), 1–32.

Bass, B. M. (1990). Transformational leadership. *Organizational Dynamics, 18*(3), 1–32.

Bennis, G. W. (2004, April). The seven ages of the leader. *The Harvard Review, 82*(1), 1–8.

Boyer, L. (2005, April/February). Supporting the induction of special educators: Program descriptions of university-school district partnerships. *Teaching Children, 37*(3) 40–50

Béland, D., & Vergniolle de Chantal, F. (2004). Fighting "big government": frames, federalism, and social policy reforming the United States. *Fighting "Big Government": frames, federalism, and social policy reforming the United States.* Advance online publication.

Capel, S. (2011). Responsibilities of subject mentors, professional mentors and link tutors in secondary physical education initial teacher education. *Mentoring and Tutoring, 11*(2), 1–23.

Contreras, R. H. (2008). *Military command-and-control leadership style and the impact of senior leader's support of mentorship* (Doctoral dissertation). Retrieved from ProQuest Theses and Dissertations database. (UMI No. 3399956)

Digest of Education Statistics 2010 [Review of the book *United States Department of Education NCES 2010-013*, by U. S. Government]. (2010).

Eby, L. T., & Allen, T. D. (2002, December). Further investigation of protégés' negative mentoring experience: patterns and outcomes. *Group and Organization Management, 27*(4), 456–480.

Fullerton, A., Ruben, B. J., McBride, S., & Bert, S. (2011, Spring). Development and design of a merged secondary and special education teacher preparation program. *Teacher Education Quarterly*, 1–43.

Gibson, D. M., & Jefferson, R. N. (2006, Spring). The effect of perceived parental involvement and the use of growth-fostering relationships on self-concept in adolescents participating in gear up. *Adolescence, 41* (161), 1–111.

Government Accounting Office. (2009). *GAO-09–946SP* (GAO-09-946SP).

Hamzah, M. I. (2010, February). Historical development of secondary education in Bangladesh: colonial period to 21st century. *International Education Studies*, 114–124.

Heavily accented teachers removed from Arizona classrooms. (2011, 2 May). *Washington Post*, 1–3. Retrieved from http://voices.washington post.com/answer-sheet/teachers/heavily-accented-teachers-remo.html

Herzberg, F. (2003, April). One more time: How do you motivate employees? *Harvard Business Review, 81*(1), 87–96.

High school graduation examination in the United States. (2011). In the United States. Retrieved from http://en.wikipedia.org/wiki/High_school _graduation_examination_in_the_United_States

Jones, M., & Straker, K. (2006, May). What informs mentors' practice when working with trainees and newly qualified teachers? An investigation into mentors' professional knowledgebase. *Journal of Education for Teaching, 1*(1), 165–185.

Juodeikaite, A., & Leliugiene, I. (2009). Non-normal education and learning from the point of view of social problems. *Social Sciences / Social Moklai, 2*(64), 1–64.

Lussier, R. N., & Achua, C. F. (2001). *Leadership: theory, application, & skill development*, Mason, OH: South-Western College Publishing.

National Center for Education Statistics [National Center for Education Statistics]. (2007–2008). *Schools and Staffing Survey (SASS, 1*(1). Retrieved from http://nces.ed.gov/pubs2009/2009320/tables/sass0708_ 2009320_d1n_07.asp

Ragins, B. R., Cotton, J. L., & Miller, J. S. (2000). Marginal mentoring:

The effects of type of mentor, quality of relationship, and program design on work and career attitudes. *Academy of Management Journal, 43*(6), 1177–1194.

Sherwin, G., & Jennings, T. (2006, September). Feared, forgotten, or forbidden: sexual orientation topics in secondary teacher preparation programs in the USA. *Teaching Education,* 207–223.

Simon, S. A. (2004, Summer). Protégés negative mentoring experiences: construct development and nomological validation. *Personnel Psychology, 57,* 2(1), 1192–1209.

Spears, L. C., & Lawrence, M. (2002). *Focus of leadership: servant-leadership for the 21st century.* New York, NY: John Wiley & Sons

Teaching in the United States. (2011). *Executive Summary* (1), 1–8.

Thomas, S., & Van Derhaar, J. (2005). Negotiating resistance to multiculturalism in a teacher education curriculum: a case study.

Troops to teachers. (2011). *Dantes* (1), 1–20.

U. S. Department of Education [Institute of Education Science]. (2010, September 2010). *WWC Intervention Report, 1*(1), 20. Retrieved from http://ies.ed.gov/ncee/wwc/pdf/wwc_ngyc_092910.pdf

Ulanoff, S. (2011). Political Interest Groups. *American Educational Research Association* (pp. 1–30). Retrieved from http://www.aera.net/Default.aspx?menu_id=26&id=274

WWC Intervention Report [National Guard Youth Challenge Program]. (2010, September). *What Works Clearinghouse,* 1–5.

Zacbary, L. J. (2000). *The mentor's guide* (1st ed.). Danvers, MA: Jossey-Bass.

About the Author

Arizona author Dr. Rene H. Contreras holds the following accredited degrees; a Bachelor of Arts (BA) from Saint Leo University, Florida; Masters of Business/Public Administration (MBA/MPA) and a Doctorate of Management (DM) in Organizational Leadership from the University of Phoenix School of Advanced Studies.

Dr. Rene enlisted in the U. S. Air Force (USAF) during his junior year in high school. As an officer, Rene's first assignment was as a technical school instructor teaching student's fighter aircraft controller serving as a rated Airborne Battle Manager. Dr. Rene and family lived overseas for nearly 19 years living in Iceland, Spain, Germany, and Alaska as part of 13 military moves which ended in 2005. After the military, Dr. Rene has been working as a Principle Systems Engineer while teaching nighttime college level courses since 1982.

In addition to publishing his doctoral dissertation, Dr. Rene has published hundreds of military, engineering technical manuals, dozens of U.S. Embassy Manuals for The U. S. Embassy Colombia in Spanish, and is currently working on a book pertaining to his military experiences.

To reach Dr. Rene H. Contreras for information on any of these topics please e-mail: ctawny01@gmail.com or caddyvibe@yahoo.com

CHAPTER 4

Evidence of Multilingual Superiority: Implications for KG–12 Curriculum

Dr. Robert D. Hobbs

Evidence with Implications for Curriculum

Transmigration has perpetuated multilingual skills throughout time, but 21st century researchers have revealed the cognitive benefits of acquiring languages (Wei, 2008). Globalization requires improved communication for diplomacy, business, media, science, and tourism at a time of diminishing natural resources (Oleksak, 2007). Conversely, curriculum in the United States lacks internationalization (Sanderson, 2008). Internationalizing post-secondary education will be the focus of this chapter.

European and Asian students are outperforming American students on the Programme for International Student Assessment (PISA) developed by the Organization for Economic Cooperation and Development (OECD) according to Schleicher (2006) and Jeynes (2008). PISA measures the success of students in secondary education for national comparisons. Schleicher (2006) explained that for every one-year increment in average education, national output increases from 3 to 6%. This statistic is an indication that educational leaders in the United States must improve education.

The problem is that students in monolingual education miss opportunities for cognitive and communicative development.

Bilingual students outperform monolingual students on cognitive judgment tasks (Bialystok, 2007). Learning three languages results in mutual acquisition reinforcement as exemplified by the Basque region of Spain (Cenoz, 2009), the Faros speaking islands of Denmark (Riemersma, 2009), the Cantonese region of Hong Kong China (Leung cited in Jessner, 2008), and other school systems involved in trilingual education (Jessner, 2006). Multilingual children demonstrated superior language accuracy in every language learned compared to bilingual children (Cenoz, 2009; Riemersma, 2009).

Outcomes of 38 studies in 20 countries demonstrated that multilingual students outperformed bilingual colleagues in higher education (Jessner, 2008). Models of curriculum design are obsolete (Bailey, Burkett, & Freeman, 2008; MacWhinney, 2008; Tyler, 2008). Thus, a well-defined model for education is needed (Conteh, 2010). The implication is that education must improve globally.

Construction of new models should incorporate findings from various branches of research. Refined neurological tools have revolutionized neurolinguistics and psycholinguistics in the knowledge of learning development. Findings in sociolinguistic research have resulted in new conceptualizations of identity and motivation (Ushioda & Dornyei, 2009). Indications from outcomes of USA terminal degree research follow.

Latino males are not persevering in schools (Alonzo, 2008) and English Speakers of Other Languages (ESOL) programs are inadequate for meeting learner needs (Chung, 2006). Alternative methods of instruction have not been explored sufficiently for L2 English learners (Goretskaya, 2006). Foreign-born Hispanics, immigrants, and minority students lag behind mainstream students (Laguerre, 2008), and college remediation placement has not succeeded (Medina, 2008). Achievement gaps between rich and poor are growing (Donlon, 2008). Perea (2009) revealed that immigrants to the United States from the Dominican Republic who accepted their bilingual identity achieved a higher proficiency in English. Students embracing their bilingual identities outperform students identifying with only one language identity. No previous studies explored the possibility of multilingual education as a solution.

Another aspect of the problem ignored by leaders is that commerce, job security, and protection of U.S. citizens is partially connected to foreign language skills (Oleksak, 2007). American competitive attitudes contrast with 88% to 95% of recruiters in Asia, Europe, and Central America who demand bilingual skills (Marshall & Heffes, 2005). English-centric policies imply that American policymakers are unaware of multilingual education advantages (Holliday, 2008). Learning languages promotes openness to cultures; multiculturalism mitigates racism, xenophobia, and ethnocentricity (Lasagabaster & Huguet, 2007).

The impact of 'one-language' policies on US businesses and US students cannot be assessed (Maclean, 2006; Salomone, 2010). No Child Left Behind (NCLB) is a disservice to 12 million immigrant learners for advocating monolingualism (Salomone, 2010). American business people (8.1 million) and American tourists (31 million) who travel internationally (Inflight Survey, 2008) would benefit by versatile language skills. Deployed US military personnel also need languages for safety and survival. According to the IRS, 1,771,803 personal 2008 tax returns were filed outside the United States in 2009 for individuals and families (IRS Research, 2010). Monolingualism compromises American economic competitiveness and national security (Demont-Heinrich, 2009). Disadvantages of English include: slang, regionalisms, chaotic spelling, and resentment of English dominance (Hurn, 2009).

Expanding languages in education could help corporate and diplomatic negotiations (Barenfanger & Tschirner, 2008). Schools of the 21st century grapple with educating multicultural, multi-ethnic, multiracial, and multilingual populations (Brinkbaumer, 2006; Burns & Roberts, 2010). Capitalizing on previous learned language experience of immigrant students in classrooms could facilitate positive language transfer to all students (Marx & Melhorn, 2010). Language policy expansion would improve American image and global competitiveness. One purpose of the Hobbs (2011) study was to construct a new model of education to incorporate the learning of languages in teacher education to cope with the diversity of student languages from kindergarten through post-secondary education.

Overview

The Hobbs (2011) study had three research questions. What theory will emerge to improve instruction and curriculum design to best facilitate multiple language acquisition and learner cognitive skill development? How should languages be systematically incorporated into the curriculum over time? What types of teaching methodologies, strategies, and techniques contribute best to construct learning, identity, intuitions, and retention of second and third languages regarding listening, speaking, reading, writing, grammar, and vocabulary?

In the pilot study macro, meso, and micro models were offered to pilot participants. Interview questions were revised from pilot participant input. Main study participants were sent questionnaires after volunteering. Repetitive themes served as suggestions for school leaders and policy makers while emerging themes indicated future research. The Hobbs (2011) study focus was on the contextual factors (macro) of learner development (meso) and the learning of languages (micro). Participants were researchers of: codeswitching (phenomenon of alternating languages), culture, curriculum, language acquisition, neurolinguistics, pragmatics, psycholinguistics, sociolinguistics, and teacher training. Every participant possessed a unique multilingual repertoire of languages.

Background

Walter (2008) reported that 42,000 children in a 20-year ongoing longitudinal study indicated that academic success is related to first language support. Multilingual education is an issue of basic linguistic human rights (Asgharzadeh, 2008; Hornberger & Hult, 2008). Monolingual English speakers outperform heritage Spanish speakers in Spanish grammar if explicit grammar instructions are not provided (Potowski, Jegershi, & Moran-Short, 2009). The implication is that L1 Spanish speakers must receive explicit L1 support.

Many bilingual students are incorrectly placed in special education because of American inefficient funding policies (Frattura & Topinka, 2006). Misdiagnosing features of accents or dialects as learning disabilities can damage motivation and perpetuate segregation, racism, and intolerance (Reaser & Adger, 2008). The resulting 'slow academic growth' and 'alienated immigrant students' are concerns related to global and national levels of policy (Hornberger & Hult, 2008).

Age of L2 and L3 language acquisition is central to developing education models. Bloch et al. (2009) considered early language learning as under the age of five years and late language acquisition as occurring after age nine. The 44 participants in the Bloch et al. (2009) study acquired L3 late. Bloch et al. (2009) explained that as the age of learning or exposure to L2 increases, an equivalent language processing network decreases. Consequently, younger exposure to L2 results in native-like acquisition. Earlier learner exposure to foreign languages would improve cognitive, metalinguistic, and communicative abilities that preclude the internationalizing of teacher post-secondary education.

Mannel and Friederici (2008) confirmed four developmental stages in psycholinguistic experiments with event related potentials (ERP). In stage one *word identification* stage, infants discriminate among phoneme parameters (sound parts) at age 2 months; later at 5 months infants recognize word stress patterns. In stage two *intonational boundary identification,* infants demonstrate sensitivity to intonation at age eight months. In stage three *lexical processing,* babies are aware of lexical form at 12 months and lexical semantics at 14 months. In stage four *sentence processing,* babies at 19 months are aware of the selection restrictions of verbs and later at 32 months toddlers begin constructing phrases.

Infant switch-task experiments revealed the influence of phonetics on language learning. Mattock, Polka, Rvachew, and Krehm (2010) stated that monolingual and bilingual infants develop adaptive speech processing skills specific to each language. Tonzar, Lotto, and Job (2009) demonstrated that learning languages together does not inflict a disadvantage. Supporting case study findings indicated that children master prosody (tonality) before they learn words (Cruz-Ferreira, 2006).

Investigating a toddler's early acquisition of three languages, Montanari (2009) studied a 24 month-old trilingual child for 2 months at age 22 months. The child was a speaker of Tagalog, Spanish, and English. Montanari (2009) explained the child could always select the appropriate language to use based on the presence of a particular speaker. The child demonstrated vocabulary gaps that caused code-switching, but alternating languages was a common family practice.

The ideal age of L2 acquisition is debated. Bloch et al. (2009) determined that brain activity variability increases in a progression from early L2 exposure to late L2 exposure. Thus, early listening to L2 causes the same brain activity as children brought up in bilingual environments. The implication is that prepubescent children should have opportunities to hear foreign languages (Missaglia, 2010). Future teachers should review L2 and L3 learning-factors in post-secondary education.

Investigators of bilingual research dispelled myths that learning L2 or L3 confuses learners (Bialystok, Craik, & Luk, 2008; Cenoz, 2009). Parents in the Basque region of Spain were initially concerned, but concern diminished when school leaders revealed that Basque children had the top scores in Spain (Lasagabaster & Sierra, 2009; Ruiz de Zarroba, Sierra, & Gallardo del Puerto, 2011). Bialystok (2005) found that both languages in bilinguals remain active in processing either language. Assertions that multiple languages may be confusing are untenable.

In theory-of-mind, mixed-cue-stimulus, and quantitative-task experiments, bilingual children consistently outperformed monolingual children. Bialystok (2005) attributed the faster performance of bilingual students in solving problems as due to superior ability of inhibiting irrelevant information distractions. The cognitive control advantages of bilinguals also protect them from cognitive decline in the aging process (Bialystok, 2007). Stafford, Sanz, and Bowden (2010) demonstrated the bilingual advantage to learning L3 persisted in late as well as early learning of L2.

Three essential factors differ between learning L2 and L3: psycholinguistic processing, sociolinguistic influence, and sequence of languages learned (Cenoz, 2009; Jessner, 2006; Safont,

2005). The main difference is that L3 learners use language learning strategies acquired in the L2 learning process. Sociolinguistic factors concerning L3 acquisition involve dominance, prestige, number of local speakers of L3, and mother tongue status. Psycholinguistic factors include cross-linguistic influences of previous languages learned, level of proficiency attained in each language, and whether the languages were learned simultaneously or in sequence as well as what age the languages were acquired. Recentness of language exposure is another influence (Bharati, 2009).

Students in trilingual language education demonstrated greater language skills than students learning two languages in every language learned in the following studies: a) French, Hebrew, English (Jessner, 2006); b) Basque, Spanish, English (Cenoz, 2009); c) Frisian, Dutch, English (Riemersma, 2009); and d) Swedish, Finnish, English (Jessner, 2006). In the Netherlands, Turkish and Moroccan immigrants performed better in learning English than Dutch monolingual students (Jessner, 2006). L3 learning reinforces language skills better than L2 learning in superior cognitive flexibility and greater repertoires of phonetic and phonological abilities that result in better pronunciation and more strategies for future language-learning (Marx & Melhorn, 2010).

Conceptual Framework

Models of education overlap several areas of theoretical investigation: neurolinguistics, psycholinguistics, pragmatics, pedagogical inquiry, policy, sociolinguistics, and other areas. The important focus here is language learning in every category. The dynamic model of multilingualism (DMM) presented by Herdina and Jessner (2002) discussed a threshold phenomenon previously explained by Cummins that stipulates that bilinguals must reach a threshold of competence and proficiency to enjoy the benefits of being bilingual (as cited in Herdina & Jessner, 2002). Learners need to reach a threshold of learning L2 for the learning investment to be advantageous for learning L3 and subsequent languages with the stipulation that L1 is maintained.

According to DMM, multilingual systems fluctuate due to language development and attrition. Language maintenance avoids language attrition. Schooling builds language skills or communicative ability dissipates. Herdina and Jessner (2002) hypothesized in DMM theory that language maintenance becomes easier for learners after developing fluency. As learners reach fluency, maintenance of a new language becomes easier. Most important, the learning of L2 increases the aptitude for learning L3, L4, L5, and subsequent languages. However, a backlash effect occurs if L1 is not maintained. If L1 is not supported, learners could develop an accent in L1 when the dominant use is in a newly acquired L2, L3, or subsequent language.

Navricsis (2007) designed research investigating 18 languages that offered support to DMM by testing how words or concepts are stored and organized in bilingual brains. The languages included in Navricsics (2007) study were: Vietnamese, Swedish, Swahili, Slovak, Serbian, Russian, Romanian, Polish, Latvian, Italian, Greek, German, French, English, Czech, Croatian, Chinese, and Arabic. Navricsics (2007) investigated four relationships: a) retrieved response correlation with word class; b) proportion of word class responses; c) meaning relationships; and d) age group responses. Navricsics (2007) monitored: nouns, verbs, infinitives, adjectives, adverbs, modifiers, pronouns, and cardinal numbers. Relationships noted were lexical equivalents (synonyms), miscellaneous, syntagmatic (word formation), hyponyms (hierarchical relationships), antonyms, collocations, meronyms (part representing whole), phrases, infinitive derivations, and semantic derivations. The findings follow.

Fluent bilingual memory storage is similar to monolinguals in the production of utterances in declarative and procedural memories. Memory storage relates more to concept than grammatical form. Navricsics (2007) findings are consistent with the explanation of declarative and non-declarative memory in Nelson, De Haan, and Thomas (2006) as well as Crowell (cited in Schumann et al, 2004). Declarative memory is also referred to as explicit memory, and non-declarative memory is the equivalent of implicit memory, as explained by Nelson et al. (2006). Post-secondary education should incorporate into curriculum how memory functions to benefit future teachers and leaders.

Syntagmatic memory precedes dual language memory. Syntagmatic storage implies that separate storage is accessible through a parallel memory search in L1 until the learner achieves native-like automatic fluency in L2. A syntagmatic representation in memory means learners must translate from L1 to L2 in early language development stages until the automaticity of fluency is achieved. Syntagmatic refers to the unconscious system of rules for syntax and lexicalization—word order and word formation (Quirk, Greenbaum, Leech, & Svartvik, 1985). The finding means that later acquisition of a language will never be incorporated into memory in the same way as L1 (Schumann et al., 2004). Thus, early exposure to foreign languages will have communicative benefits later.

Automaticity is a controversial issue. Snedeker and Thothathiri (2008) investigated semantic acquisition that involved the proposition that mapping (extrapolating rules or functions) is innate and automatic in humans. Other theories oppose the notion of innateness and automaticity. Refuting theories focus on categorizing concepts or combining semantic and syntactic connections. Psycholinguistic prosodic and semantic bootstrapping (intonation and meaning acquisition) is facilitated by the neurolinguistic function of the electrochemical circuitry of neurons, axons, and synapses as demonstrated by Booth et al. (2004), pictorialized by Foer (2007), and explained neurologically (amplitude correlated with language fluency) by Abutalebi and Della Rosa (2008). Automaticity depends on the level of proficiency attained in the target languages (Gut, 2010; Wrembl, 2010). Cross-linguistic transfer depends more on language dominance than on the length of time exposed to a foreign language (Rah, 2010).

Languages interface in the mind to offer enhanced deciphering and creative power (Singleton, 2007), so students sometimes need to speak or write in their first languages to enhance meaning-making. Teacher-understanding is necessary so students learn in their unique ways. Language abilities of multilingual students should be exploited and not shunned or inhibited. To better serve multilingual students, Cenoz (2009) advocated assessing multilingual contextual factors in every aspect of education as depicted in the continua of multilingual education model.

Perceptions vary based on language typology (Li, Dunham, & Carey, 2009). For instance, Japanese is a classifier language whereas English is a count and mass language. One example offered in the Li et al. (2009) study is the lexeme "plastic whisk." The Japanese speakers assumed the label referred to the substance *plastic,* but the English speakers assumed the label referred to the object, *whisk.* This concept is known as lexical projection. Implications are notable for learning from diversity. Teacher education should include course delivery that includes cultural linguistics. Language should not be separated from culture because languages and cultures are intrinsically linked.

How do bilinguals and multilingual speakers cognitively cope with extra languages in their minds? Bialystok (2005, 2007) and Bialystok et al. (2008) demonstrated that processing two or more languages forces the cognitive development of an inter-connectivity of linguistic rule interface manipulation to compre-hend and produce spoken or written discourse. Bialystok (2007) and Bialystok, Craik, and Ryan (2006) demonstrated that bilin-gualism has greater benefits as individuals age. Previously, Stern, Albert, Tang, and Tsai (1999) had demonstrated a corre-lation between the rate of brain degenerative decline and patient profiles of occupation and educational levels. Stern et al. (1999) suggested that *cognitive reserve* slows brain degeneration based on their discovery that greater brain density correlates with higher education and jobs requiring more cognitive intensity. Additional languages construct greater brain density for cogni-tive reserve.

Tremblay and Sabourin (2009) wrote, "Thanks to their extensive language learning experience, multilinguals develop superior learning and processing skills" (p. 75). Multilingual individuals invent appropriate language in new languages based on acquired meta-linguistic skills (Kemp, 2009). The greater cognitive flexibility of multilingualism includes more extensive parameters in the phonetic and phonological repertoire of abil-ities and potentials (Marx & Melhorn, 2010). Factors for the ways L1 and L2 influence L3 and Ln speech production and acquisition include typology (language distance from prior lan-guages learned) and language order (L1, L2, L3, Ln) or domi-nance status (Llama, Cardoso, & Collins, 2010).

Methodology

The purpose of the stratified systematic grounded theory qualitative study was to assess multilingual models of education by investigating how and when to incorporate L2 and L3 into the curriculum. The qualitative method functioned to probe participant expert experience (Moyer, 2008). Qualitative data is best for exploring expert knowledge (Codo, 2008). The grounded theory approaches selected were emerging and systematic to allow variables to emerge for constructing models or theory by systematically analyzing the data (Charmaz, 2006; Glaser & Strauss, 1967; Strauss & Corbin, 1998). Pilot participants guided the main study instrument construction. Use of the purposive sampling technique located the specialized population of researchers for pilot and main studies (Lanza, 2008).

Findings

The general problem was that monolingual educational systems hinder individual learner progress and world competitiveness (Tochon, 2009). The specific problem was that monolingual learners are deprived of opportunities to enhance critical thinking skills and communicative advantages (Cenoz, 2009; De Angelis, 2007). Teacher education would greatly benefit future learners by incorporating the advice from experts as presented in this section of findings mined from the data.

First Question Summary: When to Introduce L2 & L3?

The purpose of the study was to discover when and how to deliver languages in the curriculum. With developmental considerations, at what ages should second and third languages be introduced into the curriculum? Starting L2 and L3 in schools is context dependent. The context from the data stipulated: adequate qualified teachers, appropriate materials, and research-based methodology. Participants asserted that L2 should be taught as soon as possible or in early primary grades and L3 before age 10 or as early as possible. Only two of 13 participants (or 15%) suggested teaching L3 after age 10 by suggesting ages 13 and 15 as appropriate.

At what levels of education should second and third languages be used as the medium for delivering courses such as history, science, or math? For using L2 or L3 as a medium of instruction, most respondents offered contingent answers. The contingencies for teaching course content through a foreign language include: (a) availability of appropriate materials, methodology, and 'learning input'; (b) teacher abilities; and (c) policy. An alternative suggestion was to teach content in the language course.

Second Question Summary: What is the Greatest Impact of Research?

The second question inquired of the greatest impact of research outcomes perceived by the participants. All participants (100%) agreed that multilingual education must change. Alterations that include language learning will help more students reach post-secondary education and be more competitive after they enroll in higher education. Change in primary and secondary schools precludes change in teacher education to explain and train teachers more appropriately to deal with minority, immigrant, bilingual, and multilingual learners.

Suggestions of needed changes were similar and not discrepant. Important factors for multilingual education were: a) more funds for teacher training; b) mitigation of constraints to improve teacher skills and knowledge, develop better materials, enhance teaching methodology, and offer language teaching at appropriate frequency; c) better communication of research outcomes; d) attitude changes of educators toward minority languages to motivate learning L1, ultimately reinforcing L2 and

L3; e) funding for education reforms; f) allocation of funds for teaching, not testing because testing companies should not monopolize education. These factors comprise constraints to improving education.

All participants (100%) agreed that teacher training must improve to enhance motivation, aptitude, foreign language strategies, and linguistic awareness of learners. Improved teacher education is necessary for teachers to have a better understanding of "what learners can actually do" (participant). Teachers must: a) **use** L2 and L3 methodologies to increase metalinguistic awareness and learning flexibility; b) **create** fun activities for young learners (not formal grammar teaching); c) **link** language similarities; d) **immerse** students by teaching subjects in the target language while interacting via conversation and dialogue for comprehension; e) **allow** learners to self-correct orally, following-up individually in writing; f) **communicate** that sufficient quality sleep is essential for normal brain processing (neuroplasticity facilitates efficient learning); g) **demonstrate** the focus-on-form approach, not grammar method; and h) **demand** accuracy in the early stages of learning a language, not communicative approach.

How could attention to the theories of notional-functionalism and pragmatic-aesthetics benefit the learning of multiple languages such as offered by Saussure and further developed by Prague linguists? Two themes predominated: (a) too difficult to answer; and (b) advantageous. The advantages of notional-functional-pragmatic-aesthetics applied to multilingual education were: a) improved student metalinguistic skills; b) greater language analysis; and c) understanding of systematic language learning. One participant wrote that research into applying esthetics to curriculum has tremendous potential.

Third Question Summary: What Should All Teachers Know?

The third interview question explored what the multilingual research participants thought all teachers should know. All respondents (100%) mentioned that adequate teacher training is paramount. The specific components of teacher training should include pedagogical skills and concepts, thorough knowledge of target languages, and multilingual methodologies as well as an understanding of sociocultural and sociolinguistic contexts. Necessary pedagogical knowledge and skills included how to scaffold (arrange learning from easier to more difficult) and coordinate learning as well as respond appropriately to learners. Teachers should understand child and language development. Language knowledge should include structural and typological similarities and differences as well as fluency. Multilingual concepts needed by teachers include knowing how to bridge between languages, integrate languages in a plurilinguistic manner, and help learners draw on previous language learning. An aspect of multilingual competence includes understanding linguistic contexts, educational linguistics, adapting instruction to language background and learning styles, and differentiating between L1, L2, L3, and L4 teaching.

How has the sociolinguistic literature had an impact on your conception of multilingual education? Participants answered that sociolinguistics has had an impact on: a) public policies - political impact; b) the individual; c) perception of self; d) education; e) the immigrant, or the impact of the immigrant on the sociolinguistic environment; f) the social phenomenon aspect of sociolinguistics that focuses on what languages are used in what circumstances or locations; g) attitudes toward particular languages; and h) on language, such as the way languages change over time based on attitudes and usage.

Fourth Question Summary: How and When Should Language Group Receptivity Begin?

The predominant theme expressed was the importance of teaching language group receptivity of Slavic, Germanic, and Romance languages. Types of receptivity included the teaching of listening, reading, vocabulary, inter-comprehension and common cognates.

At what age should language group receptive skills be a part of the curriculum? Language group receptivity should begin in kindergarten or first grade by ages five or six, or as soon as possible. One participant had no opinion and another participant was not familiar with the concept of teaching 'language group receptivity.'

The rationale for including 'group language receptivity' in education is that it is much easier and faster to learn to understand languages than to speak them. Learning to understand several similar languages is extremely efficient. Teacher training would greatly benefit if teachers could learn to identify languages of students. Then, recognizing and acknowledging the languages of students in diverse classrooms would be natural. The risk of alienating 'different' students is greatly reduced by welcoming them, appreciating their heritages, assisting them in assuming the multiple identities necessary for academic success, and essential for careers that demand lifelong learning.

Conclusions: Models for Education

The purpose of the stratified systematic qualitative grounded theory study was to assess component models of education by investigating how and when to incorporate second and third languages into the curriculum to improve language acquisition. Language acquisition researchers on four continents contributed to the development of an integrated model of education. Policy makers should understand the need for curriculum adjustments in primary and secondary schools to benefit learner cognitive, meta-linguistic, analytical, and communicative abilities. Policy makers should know the benefits of providing early and continued first language support to minority students due to the synergy of mutual reinforcement and enhancement of learning three languages.

The participants who provided data for this study were researchers involved in the following areas of inquiry: applied linguistics, codeswitching, cognitive psychology, cross-cultural integration, curriculum analysis, educational theory, immigration, interdisciplinary, language education, language shift, multilingual research, neurolinguistics, pedagogy, phonology, pragmatics, program evaluation, psycholinguistics, and sociolinguistics. Participants included sequential and simultaneous learners of language. All participants have published in the English language, but English was L1 of only one participant. Participants from four continents spoke more than 18 languages (Hobbs, 2011, Table 3, p. 111). Identity is inseparable from the first language; educators honoring first languages of minority children should benefit all learners, communities, and society (Denos, Toohey, Neilson, & Waterstone, 2009; Lytra & Martin, 2010).

An Integrated Model of Education

The integrated model of multilingual education includes four models and other models that serve as tools. The four integrated models are: a) the principles of third language acquisition; b) micro model; c) meso model; and d) macro model. For each model, other models were created as tools for analyzing demographics, contextual issues, curriculum design, and future research possibilities. The following model represents the foundation of principles for the micro, meso, and macro models.

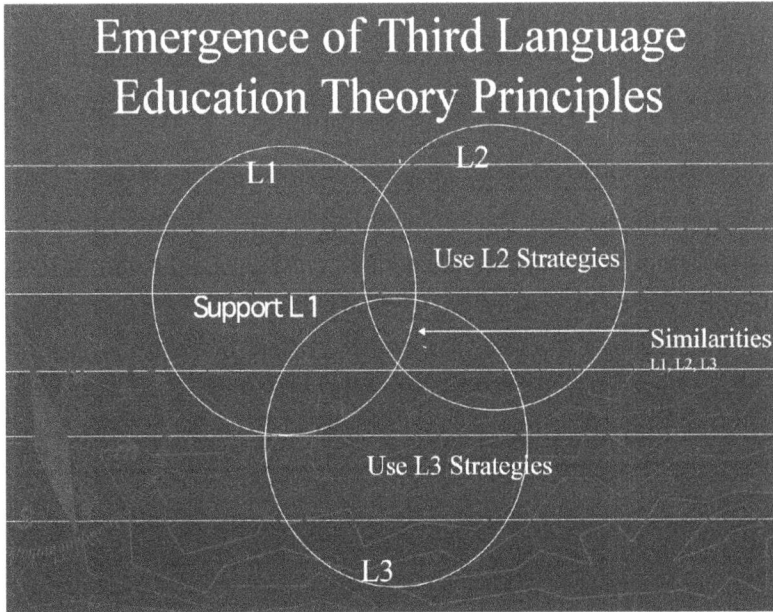

Emergence of Third Language Education Theory Principles

L1

L2

Use L2 Strategies

Support L1

Similarities
L1, L2, L3

Use L3 Strategies

L3

Figure 1. The Principles of Third Language Acquisition
(adapted from Hobbs, 2011, p. 167)

The principles of 3rd Language Acquisition emerged from the data and comprise the Venn diagram in Figure 1 that represents the development of three languages: L1, L2, and L3. First languages (L1) require support, cultural recognition, and development. Second languages (L2) require teaching to L2 principles. Third languages (L3) must be taught according to L3 principles. Teachers should teach the semantic similarities and differences (*faux ami,* false friends) of the common phonological cognates between pairs of languages. Educators must be aware of the contextual issues that influence the usage of each language, such as: location and circumstance, and L3 enhances L1 and L2 if linked and adequately supported.

The macro layer of the integrated multilingual education model was adapted from Hobbs Curriculum Framework Model (Hobbs, 2009). Seven levels (from top to bottom) of the macro model changed to reflect multiple language teaching and sociolinguistic contexts that focus on: community, school, learner, teaching, assessments, feedback, alternative assessments, and curriculum evaluation. The input (left) consists of standards, benchmarks, and performance indicators and (right) planning, monitoring, and evaluating (reads left to right). The emphasis is on the educational cycle.

The meso model consists of six overlapping dynamic spheres and an equation representing domain synergy derived from pedagogical and multilingual education literature. Participant data indicated that *Drive* (motivation) is influenced by context. *Social domain* was changed to *Contextual Domain* (larger concept) after analyzing the participant data. The meso model correlates with the multiple domain factors of bilingual and multilingual research (Safont, 2005) and explained in Hobbs (2011).

The micro model was adapted from De Bot's bilingual model that was an adaptation of Levelt's speech production model (De Angelis, 2007; Safont, 2005). The micro model depicts the language production of a multilingual mind. The domains include: cognitive, affective, psycho-motor, identity and motivation, context, and material. The implication is that identity and motivation are inseparable. Changes due to the literature research and Hobbs (2011) follow.

The changes made to the micro model due to findings in the literature include: a) language strategies and awareness increase with frequency, recency, and proficiency of exposure to other languages (Bharati, 2009); b) stimulation results in growth of neurons and synapses (Mesulam, 1999; Snell, 2010); c) comprehension is neurologically instantaneous (Pulvermuller, Shtyrov, & Hauk, 2009); d) comprehension systems include lexical access, selection, and integration (Brink & Hagoort, 2004); e) type of brain activation depends on age of language acquisition (Bloch et al, 2009); f) neural patterns in the visual cortex resemble shapes of observed objects (Damasio, 1999; Snell, 2010); g) heteromodal systems map between different representational systems (Booth et al, 2004); h) the visual search is mechanistic and computational (Taylor & Cutsuridis, in press); i) connections in the brain interface graphemic (writing), phonemic (sound), and semantic (meaning) lexicons (dictionaries in the brain) that occur in target languages stored in the brain (Schwartz, 2009); and j) nouns are produced in the sensory processing area of the brain; verbs are produced in the brain area of position and movement (Cangelosi & Parisi, 2004).

The changes made to the micro model after analyzing the participant data of Hobbs (2011) include: a) adequate sleep is required for normal brain processing (neuroplasticity); b) teacher training enhances learner Ln output; c) the comprehension system involves intercomprehension from L1, L2, L3, Ln; d) multilinguals experience plurilingual activation; and e) context influences interpretation.

Tools for the Integrated Model of Multilingualism

To enhance the integrated models, several tools were designed based on the input from the multilingual researcher participants in the study as well as the research from the literature. The tools divide into categories that correspond to each layer of the integrated model. Two macro tools are theoretical tools that apply the theories of notional functionalism and aesthetics from Saussure and the Prague Circle of linguists that are current in the literature (Mariani, 2010; Olson, 2007; Panek, 2010; Tomulet, 2010). Notional functionalism is portrayed on a continuum that traverses the continuum of aesthetic pragmatism that creates four quadrants (Hobbs, 2011). Two versions depicting this concept follow. The first tool depicts the traversing continua of the x and y axis of notional functionalism and aesthetic pragmatism (Hobbs, 2011). The second tool offers a depiction of the culminating four quadrants and suggests that each quadrant may be further investigated by particular types of inquiry (Hobbs, 2011).

Other tools provided in Hobbs (2011) study are: a) Macro Tool for Analyzing Learner Language Demographics, b) Macro Tool Explicit-Implicit Active-Passive Encoding-Decoding Analysis, c) Macro Tool for Contingency Analysis, d) Macro-Meso Tool for Learner Demographic Analysis, e) Meso Tool for Personal Heritage Student Self-Evaluation, and f) Micro Tool: Self-Evaluation of Language Ability and Mental Storage. An additional tool will be published in the *International Journal of Multilingualism* as the Curriculum Flowchart with Explicit and Implicit Instructions Applied to Notional Functional Pragmatic Aesthetic Theory (Hobbs, in press).

Findings from Hobbs (2011) suggest that notional-functionalism and aesthetic-pragmatism may present an area worthy of research. Participants claimed that notional functionalism could help students realize goals, develop pragmatic skills, improve linguistic analysis, and enhance meta-linguistic skills. Perhaps if curriculum were designed with the notional, functional, pragmatic, and aesthetic goals, multiple language learning could be improved. This notion could be combined with Bloom's taxonomy or Gardner's multiple intelligences and learning styles (Gardner, 2008). The matrix of four domains of curriculum enhancement in Hobbs (2011) offers suggestions for types of research compatible with notional, functional, pragmatic, and aesthetic aspects of curriculum. Hobbs (2012) reveals curriculum and instruction design suggestions of the curriculum cycle that follows.

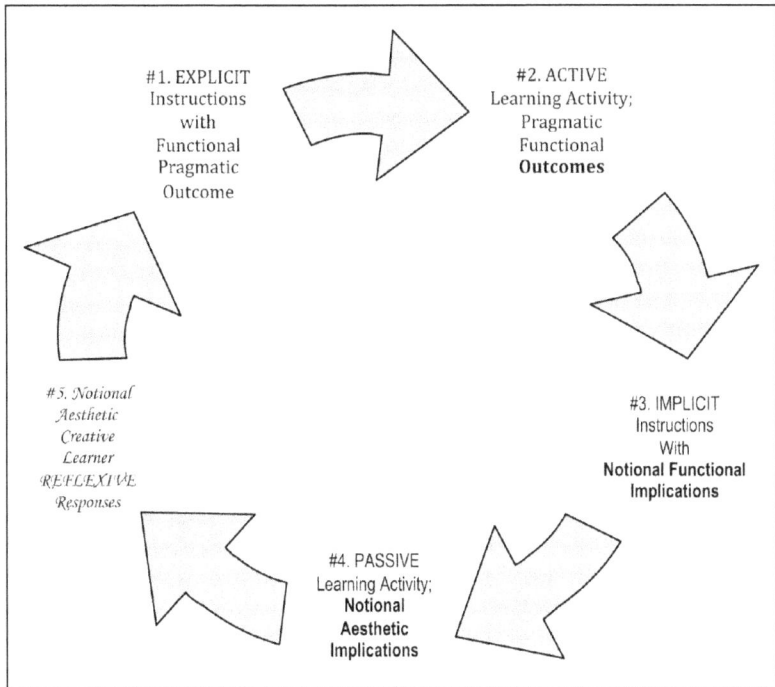

Figure 2. Notional Functional Pragmatic Aesthetic Curriculum Cycle (Hobbs, in press)

The Macro Layer of Multilingual Education Theoretical Tool for Future Research is an Intentional Paradigm of X Y Axis Interface of the Continuum of Notional Functionalism traversing the Aesthetic Pragmatic Continuum that includes four quadrants (name of quadrant depends upon location within the quadrant):

• Quadrant 1: Notional aesthetics or aesthetic notionalism;

- Quadrant 2: Functional aesthetics or aesthetic functionalism;

- Quadrant 3: Functional pragmatics or pragmatic functionalism;

- Quadrant 4: Notional pragmatics or pragmatic functionalism.

Visual explanation of notional functional pragmatic aesthetics follows.

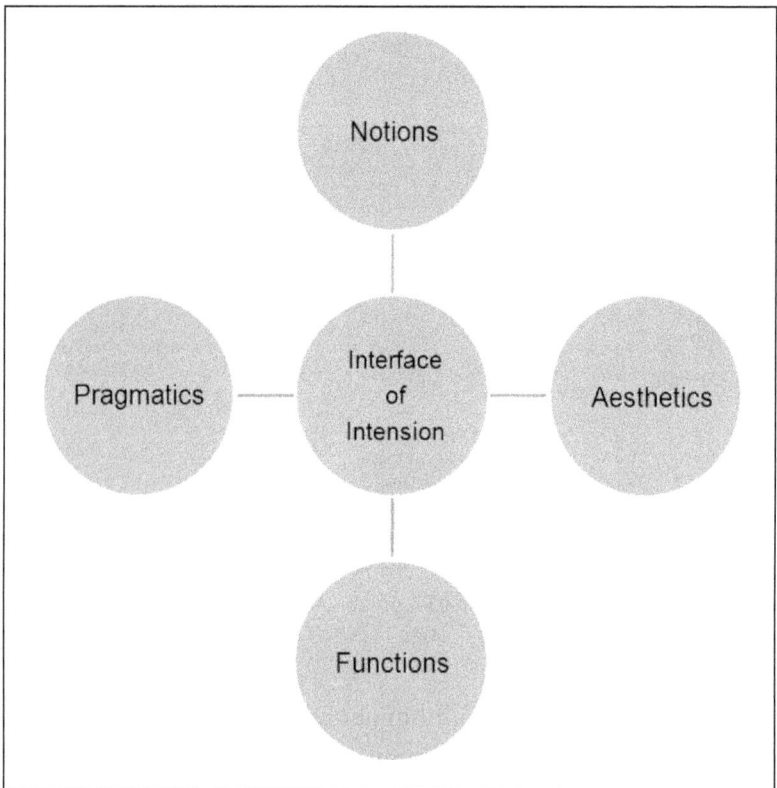

Figure 3. The model of notional functional pragmatic aesthetics
(Hobbs, 2011, p. 179)

The model of notional functional pragmatic aesthetics (Figure 3) is a macro tool for designing curriculum. The implicit equation is: Intentional Paradigm of X Y Axis = Continuum of Notional Functionalism x Aesthetic Pragmatic Continuum = 4 quadrants. The implication is that projects and lesson plans should consider the elements of assignments that are functional, pragmatic, notional, and aesthetic. The interface is of intension (intensity) and intention (what was intended).

Notional and aesthetic curriculum enhancements and outcomes require qualitative investigation. Functional outcomes require quantitative investigation. Pragmatics requires an improvement to function, so requires mixed method research. Teacher professional development should include explanations of reading and writing activity delineations as: a) explicit-active; b) explicit-passive; c) implicit-active; d) implicit-passive. Examples of human cultural products for each quadrant follow:

Quadrant 1 Notional Aesthetics: musical composition, lyrics, literature, dance, artistic expression, poetry, sculpting, painting;

Quadrant 2 Functional Aesthetics: architectural rendering, pottery, tapestry, clothing, transportation, modality, shelter, furnishing, cuisine presentation;

Quadrant 3 Functional Pragmatism: engines, electronics, computer hardware, machinery, robotics, utilitarian prosthetics, minimalist desk and chair, shelves and filing cabinets, instructions;

Quadrant 4 Notional Pragmatism: computer software, accounting setup, investment portfolio, dietary variation, memos, recipes, formal and informal communication.

At the processing level, notional functionalism and aesthetic pragmatism could offer opportunities to design studies to measure the impact of offering tasks to participants that stimulate the creative aspect of language production via notional and aesthetic cues versus pragmatic functional cues. Studies could be designed to test if creative and notional cues in combination with pragmatic functional cues stimulate greater learning than tasks isolated in the creative notional or pragmatic functional directions.

Learning multiple languages should improve communication and metacognitive skills as well as contribute to enhancing the ambiance of multicultural schools. Tolerance of difference should be facilitated. Empathy toward immigrants learning the dominant language should improve as students who speak the dominant language as a mother tongue struggle to improve their foreign language skills.

Vast improvement in brain scanning technology has offered neurolinguists and psycholinguists better equipment for doing research. The assertion that syntax can be correlated with synaptic and neuronal activation is unique to this study and deserves further investigation in neurolinguistic research for intervention studies. Another implication in the literature is that vocal tonality may be correlated with syntax assimilation and could be useful as a teaching strategy. Incorporating foreign language instruction into post-secondary education for teachers and international business majors has tremendous potential for improving global communication, commercial competitiveness, and diplomatic cooperation.

REFERENCES

Abutalebi, J., & Della Rosa, P. (2008). Imaging technologies. In L. Wei & M. Moyer (Eds.), *The Blackwell guide to research methods in bilingualism and multilingualism* (pp. 132–157). Oxford, UK: Blackwell Publishing.

Alonzo, V. (2008). *Predicting Latino males' persistence from high school: A model combining social and academic risk factors.* (Doctoral dissertation). Available from ProQuest Dissertations and Theses database. (UMI No: 3324061)

Asgharzadeh, A. (2008). The return of the subaltern: International education and politics of voice. *Journal of Studies in International Education, 12,* 334–363. doi: 10.1177/1028315307308137

Bailey, F., Burkette, B., & Freeman, D. (2008). The mediating role of language in teaching and learning: A classroom perspective. In B. Spolsky & F. Hult (Eds.), *The handbook of educational linguistics* (pp. 606–625). Oxford, UK: Blackwell Publishing Ltd.

Barenfanger, O., & Tschirner, E. (2008). Language education policy and language learning quality management: The common European framework of reference. *Foreign Language Annals, 41*(1), 81–102.

Bharati, S. (2009, September). *Phonological awareness of learners of English as an L3.* Paper presented at the Sixth International Conference on Third Language Acquisition and Multilingualism, Free University of Bolzano, Italy.

Bialystok, E. (2005). Consequences of bilingualism for cognitive development. In J. Kroll & A. De Groot (Eds.), *Handbook of bilingualism* (pp. 417–422). Oxford, UK: Oxford University Press.

Bialystok, E. (2007). Cognitive effects of bilingualism: How linguistic experience leads to cognitive change. *International Journal of Bilingual Education & Bilingualism, 10*(3), 210–223. doi: 10.2167/beb441.0

Bialystok, E., Craik, F., & Luk, G. (2008). Cognitive control and lexical access in younger and older bilinguals. *Journal of Experimental Psychology: Learning, Memory, and Cognition, 34*(4), 859–873. doi:10.1037/0278-7393.34.4.859

Bialystok, E., Craik, F., & Ryan, J. (2006). Executive control in a modified antisaccade task: Effects of aging and bilingualism. *Journal of Experimen-*

tal Psychology: Learning, Memory, and Cognition, 32(6), 1341–1354. doi:10.1037/0278-7393.32.6.1341

Bloch, C., Kaiser, A., Kuenzli, E., Zappatore, D., Haller, S., Francschini, R. . . . Nitsch,C. (2009). The age of second language acquisition determines the variability in activation elicited by narration in three languages in Broca's and Wernicke's area. *Neuropsychologia, 47*, 625–633.

Booth, J., Burman, D., Meyer, J., Gitelman, D., Parrish, T., & Mesulam, M. (2004). Development of brain mechanisms for processing orthographic and phonologic representations. *Journal of Cognitive Neuroscience, 16* (7), 1234–1249.

Brink, D., & Hagoort, P. (2004). The influence of semantic and syntactic context constraints on lexical selection and integration in spoken-word comprehension as revealed by ERP's (Event Related Potential). *Journal of Cognitive Neuroscience, 16*(6), 1068–1084.

Brinkbaumer, K. (2006). Die neue Volkerwanderung; Welt der wandern- den. *Der Spiegel, 26*, 66–70. [The new migrants; World of immigrants. *Der Spiegel* means *The Mirror.*]

Burns, A., & Roberts, C. (2010). Migration and adult language learning: Global flows and local transpositions. *TESOL Quarterly, 44*(3), 409–419.

Cangelosi, A., & Parisi, D. (2004). The processing of verbs and nouns in neural networks: Insights from synthetic brain imaging. *Brain and Language, 89*, 401–408.

Cenoz, J. (2009). Towards multilingual education; Basque educational research from an international perspective. Bristol, UK: Multilingual Matters.

Charmaz, K. (2006). *Constructing grounded theory; A practical guide through qualitative analysis.* London, UK: Sage Publications Ltd.

Chung, G. (2006). *English for speakers of other language programs' effect on high school graduation and college plans.* (Doctoral dissertation). Available from ProQuest Dissertations and Theses database. (UMI No: 3245545)

Codo, E. (2008). Interviews and questionnaires. In L. Wei & M. Moyer (Eds.), *The Blackwell guide to research methods in bilingualism and mul- tilingualism* (pp. 158–176). Oxford, UK: Blackwell Publishing.

Conteh, J. (2010). Making links across complementary and mainstream classrooms for primary children and their teachers. In V. Lytra & P. Martin (Eds.), *Sites of multilingualism; Complementary schools in Britain today* (pp. 149–160). Stoke on Trent, UK: Trentham Books.

Cruz-Ferreira, M. (2006). *Three is a crowd? Acquiring Portuguese in a trilingual environment.* Bristol, UK: Multilingual Matters.

Damasio, A. (1999). How the brain creates the mind. *Scientific American, 281*(6), 112.

De Angelis, G. (2007). *Third or additional language acquisition.* Clevedon, UK: Multilingual Matters Ltd.

Demont-Heinrich, C. (2009). Globalization, language, and tongue-tied American; A textual analysis of American discourses on the global hegemony of English. *Journal of Communication Inquiry, 31*(2), 98–117. doi: 10.1177/0196859906298117.

Denos, C., Toohey, K., Neilson, K., & Waterstone, B. (2009). *Collaborative research in multilingual classrooms.* Bristol, UK: Multilingual Matters.

Donlon, J. (2008). *Alternative education: Understanding program effectiveness to meet the needs of at-risk youth.* (Doctoral dissertation, University of Phoenix, 2008). UMI no. 3323346.

Foer, J. (2007). Remember this. *National Geographic, 212*(5), 32–57.

Fratura, E., & Topinka, C. (2006). Theoretical underpinnings of separated educational programs: The social justice challenge continues. *Education and Urban Society, 38,* 327–344. doi: 10.1177/001312450 6287032

Gardner, H. (2008). *Five minds for the future.* Boston, MA: Harvard Business Press.

Glaser, B., & Strauss, A. (1967). *The discovery of grounded theory: Strategies for qualitative research.* Piscataway, NJ: Transaction Publishers.

Goretskaya, Y. (2006). *Influence of alternative methods of instruction on English learners' achievements in northern California school districts.* (Doctoral dissertation). Available from ProQuest Dissertations and Theses database. (UMI No: 3251379)

Gut, U. (2010). Cross-linguistic influence in L3 phonological acquisition. *International Journal of Multilingualism, 7*(1), 19–38.

Herdina, P., & Jessner, U. (2002). *A dynamic model of multilingualism: Perspectives of change in psycholinguistics.* Clevedon, UK: Multilingual Matters.

Hobbs, R. (2009). The Hobbs report on educational excellence: Reflective value, redirection, and a way forward. In *AUK Occasional Papers; Liberal Arts &Business Affairs, No. 3.* (pp. 94–102). Kuwait: American University of Kuwait.

Hobbs, R. (2011). *Multilingual education model construction based on superior cognitive skills of multilingual students.* (unpublished doctoral dissertation). University of Phoenix, Phoenix, AZ.

Hobbs, R. (2012). Can trilingualism be the pathway to improve bilingualism? Submitted to: The Braziliam Immersion Conference for Educators, Sao Paulo, Brazil.

Hobbs, R. (in press). Diverse multilingual researchers contribute language acquisition components to an integrated model of education. *International Journal of Multilingualism.* DOI:10.1080/14790718.2011.630736

Holliday, A. (2008). Standards of English and politics of inclusion. *Language Teaching, 41*(1), 119–130.

Hornberger, N., & Hult, F. (2008). Ecological language education policy. In B. Spolsky & F. Hult (Eds.), *The handbook of educational linguistics* (pp. 280–296). Oxford, UK: Blackwell Publishing Ltd.

Hurn, B. (2009). Will international business always speak English? *Industrial and Commercial Training, 41*(6), 299–304. doi: 10.1108/00197850910983884

Inflight Survey (2008). Profile of U.S. resident travelers visiting overseas destinations: 2007 Outbound. U.S. Department of Commerce. International Trade Administration. Manufacturing and Services. Office of Travel and Tourism Industries.

IRS Research (2010, March). Number of returns filed by type of return and state, fiscal year 2009 (Table 3). Research, Analysis, and Statistics, Office of Research. Internal Revenue Service.

Jessner, U. (2006). Linguistic awareness in multilinguals: English as a third language. Edinburgh, UK: Edinburgh University Press.

Jessner, U. (2008). Teaching third languages: Findings, trends and challenges. *Language Teaching, 41*(1), 15–56.

Jeynes, W. (2008). What we should and should not learn from the Japanese and other East Asian education systems. *Educational Policy, 22,* 900–927. doi: 10.1177/0895904807310042.

Kemp, C. (2009, September). *Learning, transfer, and creativity in multilingual language learning: A dynamic systems approach.* Paper presented at the Sixth International Conference on Third Language Acquisition and Multilingualism, Free University of Bolzano, Italy.

Laguerre, P. (2008). *A case study of foreign-born Hispanic students in community college.* (Doctoral dissertation) Available from ProQuest Dissertations and Theses database. (UMI No:3337536)

Lanza, E. (2008). Selecting individuals, groups, and sites. In L. Wei & M. Moyer (Eds.), *The Blackwell guide to research methods in bilingualism and multilingualism,* (pp. 73–87). Oxford, UK: Blackwell Publishing.

Lasagabaster, D., & Huguet, A., (Eds.) (2007). Multilingualism in European countries. Clevedon, UK: Multilingual Matters.

Lasagabaster, D., & Sierra, J. (2009). Language attitudes in CLIL and traditional EFL classes. *International CLIL Research Journal, 1*(2), 4–17.

Li, P., Dunham, Y., & Carey, S. (2009). Of substance: The nature of language effects on identity construal. *Cognitive Psychology, 58,* 487–524.

Llama, R., Cardoso, W., & Collins, L. (2010). The influence of language distance and language status on the acquisition of L3 phonology. *International Journal of Multilingualism, 7*(1), 39–57.

Lytra, V., & Martin, P. (Eds.), (2010). *Sites of multilingualism; Complementary schools in Britain today.* Stoke on Trent, UK: Trentham Books.

Maclean, D. (2006). Beyond English; Transnational corporations and the strategic management of language in a complex multilingual business environment. *Management Decision, 44*(10), 1377–1390. doi:10.1108/002517 40610715704

MacWhinney, B. (2008). A unified model. In P. Robinson & N. Ellis (Eds.), *Handbook of cognitive linguistics and second language acquisition* (pp. 341–371). New York, NY: Routledge.

Mannel, C., & Friederici, A. (2008). Event-related brain potentials as a window to children's language processing; From syllables to sentences. In I. Sekerina, E. Fernandez, & H. Clahsen (Eds.), *Developmental psycholinguistics; On-line methods in children's language processing: Language Acquisition & Language Disorders, 44* (pp. 29–72). Amsterdam: John Benjamins Publishing Company.

Mariani, A. (2010). *The unconscious on the stage in the theatrical productions of Luigi Antonelli, Luigi Prandello e the "Grotesques"*. (Doctoral dissertation, Rutgers State University of New Jersey–New Brunswick, 2010). Available from ProQuest Dissertations and Theses. (UMI No: 3397503)

Marshall, J., & Heffes, E. (2005). Multilingual executives preferred: Recruiters. *Financial Executive, 21*(3), 10.

Marx, N., & Melhorn, G. (2010). Pushing the positive: Encouraging phonological transfer from L2 to L3. *International Journal of Multilingualism, 7*(1), 4–18.

Mattock, K., Polka, L., Rvachew, S., & Krehm, M. (2010). The first steps in word learning are easier when the shoes fit: Comparing monolingual and bilingual infants. *Developmental Science, 13*(1), 229–243.

Medina, M. (2005). A case study: Progress of limited English proficient students in a community setting. (Doctoral dissertation). Available from ProQuest Dissertations and Theses database. (UMI no: 3327212)

Mesulam, M. (1999). Neuroplasticity failure in Alzheimer's Disease: Bridging the gap between plaques and tangles. *Neuron, 24,* 524–529.

Missaglia, F. (2010). The acquisition of L3 English vowels by infant German-Italian bilinguals. International Journal of Multilingualism, 7(1), 58–74.

Montanari, S. (2009). Pragmatic differentiation in early trilingual development. *Journal of Child Language, 36,* 597–627.

Moyer, M. (2008). Research as practice: Linking theory, method, and data. In Li Wei & M. Moyer (Eds.), *The Blackwell guide to research methods in bilingualism and multilingualism* (pp. 18–31). Oxford, UK: Blackwell Publishing.

Navracsics, J. (2007). Word classes and the bilingual mental lexicon. In Z. Langyal & J. Navracsics (Eds.), *Second language lexical processes; Applied linguistic and psycholinguistic perspectives* (pp. 17–35). Clevedon, UK: Multilingual Matters.

Nelson, C., De Haan, M., & Thomas, K. (2006). *Neuroscience of cognitive development: The role of experience and the developing brain.* Hoboken, NJ: John Wiley & Sons, Inc.

Oleksak, R. (2007). Ensuring America's place in the global economy by building language capacity in the schools. *Foreign Language Annals, 40*(1), 5.

Olson, J. (2007). *The romantic poet in modern garb: Four interpretations of Karel Hynek Macha and Mikhail Iurevich Lermontov during the interwar period*. (Doctoral dissertation). Available from ProQuest Dissertations and Theses database. (UMI No: NR39667)

Panek, M. (2010). *The postmodern treatment of myth in the writings of Michel Tournier*. (Doctoral dissertation, Catholic). Available from ProQuest Dissertations and Theses database. (UMI No: 3391290)

Perea, F. (2009). *Academic performance among children of immigrant families from the Dominican Republic: The influence of language*. (Doctoral dissertation). Available from ProQuest Dissertations and Theses database. (UMI no: 3342169)

Potowski, K., Jegerski, J., & Morgan-Short, K. (2009). The effects of instruction on linguistic development in Spanish heritage language speakers. *Language Learning, 59*(3), 537–579.

Pulvermuller, F., Shtyrov, Y., & Hauk, O. (2009). Understanding in an instant: Neurophysiological evidence for mechanistic language circuits in the brain. *Brain and Language, 110*, 81–94.

Quirk, R., Greenbaum, S., Leech, G., & Svartvik, J. (1995). *A comprehensive grammar of the English language*. London, UK: Longman.

Rah, A. (2010). Transfer in L3 sentence processing: Evidence from relative clause attachment ambiguities. *International Journal of Multilingualism, 7*(2), 147–161.

Reaser, J., & Adger, C. (2008). Vernacular language varieties in educational settings: Research and development. In B. Spolsky & F. Hult (Eds.), *The handbook of educational linguistics* (pp. 161–173). Oxford, UK: Blackwell Publishing Ltd.

Riemersma, A. (2009, September). *Trilingual schooling in Frysian: Results and challenges*. Sixth International Conference on Third Language Acquisition and Multilingualism, Free University of Bolzano, Italy.

Ruiz de Zarobe, Y., Sierra, J., & Gallardo del Puerto, F. (2011). *Content and foreign language integrated learning*. Berlin, Germany: Peter Lang International Academic Publishers.

Safont, M. (2005). *Third language learners; Pragmatic production and awareness*. Toronto, Canada: Multilingual Matters Ltd.

Salomone, R. (2010). True American: Language, identity, and the education of immigrant children. Boston, MA: Harvard University Press.

Sanderson, G. (2008). A foundation for the internationalization of the academic self. *Journal of Studies in International Education, 12,* 276–307.

Schleicher, A. (2006). Divided Europe; A classless act. *Newsweek Special Edition,* 96–97.

Schumann, J., Crowell, S., Jones, N., Lee, N., Schuchert, S., & Wood, L. (2004). *The neurobiology of learning; Perspectives from second language acquisition.* London, UK: Lawrence Erlbaum Associates, Publishers.

Schwartz, R. (Ed.). (2009). *Handbook of child language disorders.* New York, NY: Psychology Press.

Singleton, D. (2007). How integrated is the integrated mental lexicon? In Lenyal, Z., & Navracsics, J. (Eds.), *Second language lexical processes; Applied linguistics and psycholinguistic perspectives* (pp. 3–16). Clevedon, UK: Multilingual Matters.

Snedeker, J., & Thothathiri, M. (2008). What lurks beneath; Syntactic priming during language comprehension in preschoolers (and adults). In I. Sekerina, E. Fernandez, & H. Clahsen (Eds.), *Developmental psycholinguistics; On-line methods in children's language processing: Language Acquisition & Language Disorders, 44* (pp. 137–167). Amsterdam, Netherlands: John Benjamins Publishing Company.

Snell, R. (2010). *Clinical neuroanatomy (7th ed.).* New York, NY: Wolters Kluwer Lippincott Williams & Wilkins.

Stafford, C., Sanz, C., & Bowden, H. (2010). An experimental study of early L3 development: Age, bilingualism, and classroom exposure. *International Journal of Mulilingualism, 7*(2), 162–183.

Stern, Y., Albert, S., Tang, M., & Tsai, W. (1999). Rate of memory decline in AD is related to education and occupation; Cognitive reserve? *Neurology, 53*(9), 1942–1947.

Strauss, A., & Corbin, J. (1998). *Basics of qualitative research: Techniques and procedures for developing grounded theory (2nd ed.).* Los Angeles, CA: Sage.

Taylor, J., & Cutsuridis, V. (in press). Saliency, attention, active visual search and picture scanning. *Cognitive Computation.*

Tochon, F. (2009). The key to global understanding: World languages education—why schools need to adapt. *Review of Educational Research, 79*(2), 650–681. doi: 10.3102/0034654308325898.

Tomulet, D. (2010). *Being and sign in the "Enneads".* (Doctoral dissertation). Available from ProQuest Dissertations and Theses database. (UMI No: 3399134)

Tonzar, C., Lotto, L., & Job, R. (2009). L2 vocabulary acquisition in children: Effects of learning method and cognate status. *Language Learning, 59*(3), 623–646.

Tremblay, M., & Sabourin, L. (2009, September). *Comparing the perceptual abilities of monolinguals, bilinguals, and multilinguals: Methodological issues.* Paper presented at the Sixth International Conference on Third Language Acquisition and Multlingualism, Free University of Bolzano, Italy.

Tyler, A. (2008). Cognitive linguistics and second language instruction. In P. Robinson & N. Ellis (Eds.), *Handbook of cognitive linguistics and second language acquisition* (pp. 456–488). New York, NY: Routledge.

Ushioda, E., & Dornyei, Z. (2009). Motivation, language identities and the L2 self: A theoretical overview. In Z. Dornyei & E. Ushioda (Eds.) *Motivation, language identity and the L2 self* (pp. 1–8). Bristol, UK: Multilingual Matters.

Walter, S. (2008). The language of instruction issue: Framing an empirical perspective. In B. Spolsky & F. Hult (Eds.), *The handbook of educational linguistics* (pp. 129–146). Oxford, UK: Blackwell Publishing.

Wei, L. (2008). Research perspectives on bilingualism and multilingualism. In L. Wei & M. Moyer (Eds.), *The Blackwell guide to research methods in bilingualism and multilingualism.* Oxford, UK: Blackwell Publishing.

Wrembl, M. (2010). L2-accented speech in L3 production. *International Journal of Multilingualism, 7*(1), 75–90.

About the Author

Dr. R. D. Hobbs earned a Bachelor of Arts (BA) from Marshall University in Huntington, West Virginia; Master of Education (M Ed) from the Mililani Campus Honolulu branch of the University of Phoenix; and Doctorate of Curriculum and Instruction (Ed D) from the University of Phoenix School of Advanced Studies. He has computer certification from Atlanta Tech, teacher certification from the State of Hawaii, and Recognition of Excellence from the Educational Testing Service (ETS) for his performance on the national teacher exam in Assessing Language Production, Behavioral Sciences, Economics, Linguistic Theory, and Social Studies.

Scholarly writings by Dr. Hobbs include: "Diverse multilingual researchers contribute language acquisition components to an integrated model of education" (*International Journal of Multilingualism*); "The Hobbs Report on Educational Excellence" (Middle East Liberal Arts Conference, AUK); *Multilingual Education Model Construction Based on Superior Cognitive Skills of Multilingual Students* (UOP); *Curriculum Innovation Implementation of Systemic Change* (JCSC Ministry of Defense); and *Theory, Practice, and Pedagogical Compilation of a Didactic ESP Glossary* (Freie University Berlin).

Dr. Robert Hobbs, member of TESOL Arabia, has designed curriculum, taught, and supervised academic writing, business English, biology, educational psychology, geography, history, investment banking, tax law, oral presentations, teacher professional development, and TOEFL in public and private sectors in Atlanta, Tokyo, Prague, Berlin, Luxembourg, Honolulu, Dubai, and Kuwait at 6 higher education institutions and K-12 in the USA, Europe, Asia, and the Middle East.

His next publication is *Jump-Start Genius: The Hobbs Report for Parents, Teachers, and Mentors*.

Dr. Robert Hobbs can be reached by email at: robertdeanhobbs@hotmail.com

CHAPTER 5

A Contextual Applied Research Analysis of Negative Public Perceptions

Dr. Emad Rahim and
Dr. Darrell Norman Burrell

Negative public perception can be seen as the difference between an absolute truth based on facts and a perceived potentially false truth shaped by popular opinion, media coverage, or even reputation. While organizations may strive to do the right things for the right reasons, public perception can make the achievement of organizational goals more complex (Hakanson, 1981). In the realm of public perception, a labeling phenomenon is taking shape within inner-city community-based organizations, also known as community centers and organizations. These urban community centers have been labeled as 'ghetto' agencies. To explore this phenomenon, researchers interviewed volunteers to discern whether the services available matched the community needs of the clients (Rahim, 2010). A consistent theme emerged with negative perceptions about the quality of service and absence of professionalism on the part of staff paralleled the use of terms such as 'being ghetto' or 'acting too ghetto' from clients and other members in the community. This feedback warranted further inquiry due to the significant nature of the socialization and assisting activities offered by these organizations, including afterschool programs, workforce development training, public health education training, and counseling services. The concern was that the label of 'ghetto,' negative stigmas, and pessimistic perceptions might hamper the most vulnerable and needy in the community from accessing services that could be beneficial in four community centers in Syracuse, New York and discover new perspectives for furthering this research topic.

Community development in community centers occurs as residents use the resources and expertise of the organizations to take responsibility for managing their own problems. Taking responsibility includes identifying problems, developing actions, putting them into place, and following them through accordingly (Cheetham, 2002). Hence, the roles of participation in community development and public image are very important in terms of the credibility of these community centers and the services they provide. Community development cannot take place if there is no participation by the community and if the perception of the organization is negative. Historically, all of these community centers depended on support by larger corporations to underwrite their fund-raising campaigns and community programs to stay fiscally prudent. Access to this funding depends on the level of esteem that these organizations hold in the community. Corporations, grantees, and other donors want to be connected to organizations with solid reputations for great work and quality services (Ewen & Ewen, 2006). The impacts of these negative labels is that all of these agencies have experienced a drastic decrease in funding support and have lost a significant amount of programs, services, and jobs.

The 2010 Rahim research study employed cooperative research methods to retrieve relevant information. We interviewed various individuals within non-profit social services agencies, who can use the information to develop policy changes, action steps, or procedures to mitigate or eliminate problems within the agency. In addition, this 2010 Rahim ethnographic study of these community agencies provides the empirical frame for an examination of the social production of the ethnographer from the informants' point of view.

This social services agencies study explored the issue through three primary research questions:

1. What is responsible for the stigmatization of community agencies as 'ghetto,' and how does this stigmatization occur?

2. What are the implications for community agencies labeled as 'ghetto'?

3. What are strategies and solutions for community agencies to counteract the negative effects of being stigmatized as 'ghetto'?

The Rahim and Burrell 2010 study also investigated the problem of stigmatization for community organizations by drawing on the seminal theories of Cooley (1902), Lewin (1958), G. H. Mead (1934, 1938), Goffman (1959, 1963), and Okhuysen and Hudson (2003), and Hudson (2008). Furthermore, the researchers offered strategies and solutions for organizations stigmatized as 'ghetto' based on the interplay of the work by the theorists stated above in the context of the results of this applied research study.

The Rahim and Burrell 2010 study provides a view of the causal relationship of negative labeling from the framework of Capra's (2003) conceptualization of living systems. Building, among others, on the work of Maturana and Varela (1987) in biology, and Luhmann (1990) in social science, Capra (2003) defined living systems as self-generating networks. In this way living networks undergo continual structural changes while preserving their web-like patterns of organization. Basic living structures, such as cells, exist far from thermodynamic equilibrium and would soon decay toward equilibrium (i.e., interconnected systems rely on each other or they would die) if they did not use a continual flow of energy to restore structures as fast as they are decaying. Capra identifies three aspects of living systems: pattern, structure, and process. In social systems (in contrast to living systems), there is a fourth aspect: meaning, which refers to the inner world of reflective consciousness (Capra, 2003) (see Figure 1).

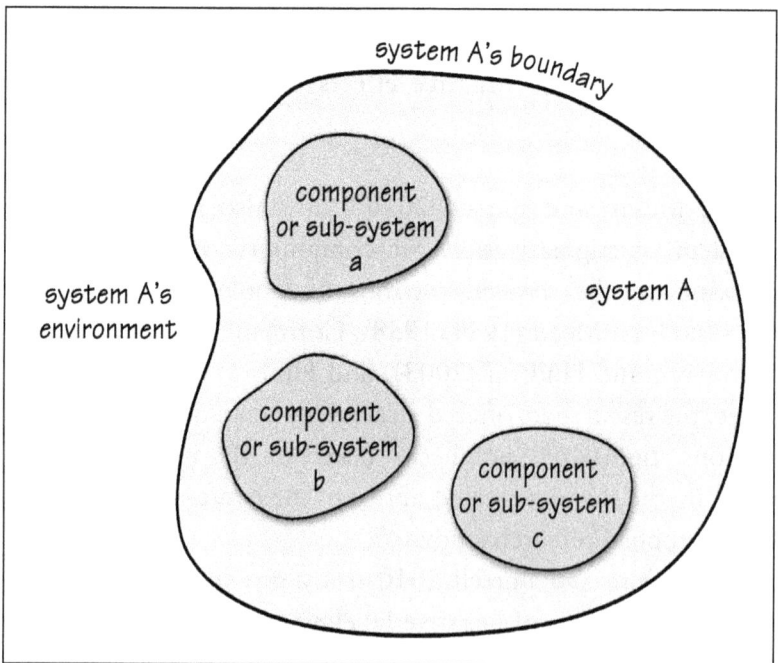

Figure 1: Interconnected Systems Diagram Provides a Visual Depiction of Capra's Perspective.

French and Bell (1979) in their classic 'Iceberg Model' (see Figure 2) demonstrate the behavioral, cognitive, and emotional components of people (management, staff, clients), their cultures, and interrelated nature of their interactions and perceptions. On this basis, Altman and Taylor (1973) synthesized as a definition of culture "the set of knowledge, values, emotional heritage, behavior and artifacts which a social group share, and which enable them to functionally adapt to their surroundings" (p.73). Thus, culture affects us in the way we interact with our environment (Schoem, 1991). If we understand culture and how it is viewed, then we can understand how an organizational culture viewed as 'ghetto and unprofessional' could be less effective in meeting its mission or serving its stakeholders.

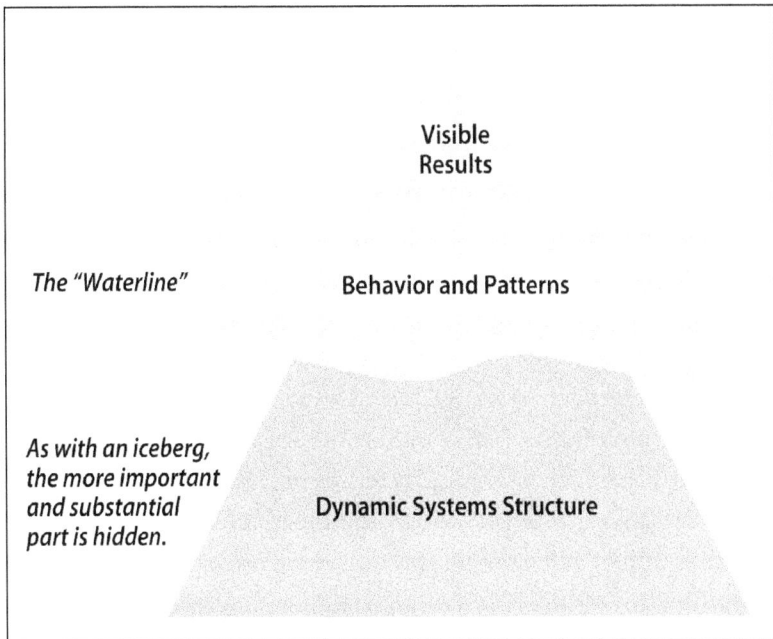

**Visible
Results**

The "Waterline"   **Behavior and Patterns**

*As with an iceberg,
the more important
and substantial
part is hidden.*   **Dynamic Systems Structure**

Figure 2: Iceberg Figure of Systems Perspectives.

Self-Development and the Operation of Stereotypes

The 'looking glass-self,' a concept created by Charles Cooley (1902), asserts that individuals learn to see themselves based on how society views them; individuals take on characteristics that are predominately influenced by what we believe society perceives us to be. Under this theory, stereotyped individuals come to integrate society's label of them as their identity, and reproduce behaviors associated with that identity. Cooley's theory and the behaviors and attitudes of marginalized people living in the ghetto share many aspects. People who live in underprivileged neighborhoods (the 'ghetto') are frequently negatively stereotyped and labeled, often leading people to think poorly of themselves and their opportunities Cooley, 1902). According to Cooley (1902) there is a strong correlation between the 'looking glass-self' and the influences of social stereotypes on the development of the 'self.' Stereotypes are seen as negative labeling, while the 'looking glass-self' is viewed more as a normal experience we all go through in discovering who we really are. The 'looking glass-self' seems to question whether individualism is truly gained by social influences on the 'self.' Exploring Cooley's perspectives provides a framework that outline how the same phenomenon can occur with regard to how stereotypes and labeling influence how marginalized people see themselves.

George Herbert Mead (1934, 1938), a follower of Cooley (1902), contended that it as unfeasible for anyone to conceive a self in the absence of social interaction. Mead postulated an understanding of the self as inter-subjective, believing that the self was constructed in interaction with others through such mechanisms as social control, roles, and the generalized other. Mead supported and developed Cooley's (1902) theory that individuals tend to represent their identities as perceived by others. However, going beyond perception, Mead's theory specifies that the understandings of the self, and the accompanying behaviors of that self, are solidified through the experiences gained in the interactions with people (Mead, 1938). Mead (1934, 1938) had a devoutly pragmatic attitude toward identity formation, and believed that an individual existed as a part of a community before existing with individual consciousness (Joas, 1985). Mead postulated that only through experience with different communities can individuals become self-aware. This construct is important in explaining the persistent negative stigmatization of community agencies as 'ghetto.'

Mead (1982) also forwarded the concept of 'the generalized other,' which is essentially a summation of the social norms in a given community or environment. Mead's (1934, 1982) important contribution to this research is in framing the elements of the agency that carry the negative stigmatization of being 'ghetto,' which reflects on the organization. The employees and clients who are stereotyped as being 'ghetto' can be understood as a clashing of perceptions of 'the generalized other.' The key element here is the experience of those involved, which can be intrinsically tied to education and opportunity, both of which are lacking in disenfranchised areas.

Erving Goffman (1959, 1963) affirmed Mead's (1934, 1938) argument that the identity of an individual is constructed through an understanding of the projection of the self to others. Goffman posited that individuals will go to great lengths to combat a stigma they feel is attached to them, and in doing so, may work to reinforce that stigma.

Labeling and Stereotypes

Sociologist David Schoem (1991) defined stereotyping as a set of generalizations held by one group of people regarding the characteristics and behaviors of a different group based on an image or assumption, instead of sound evidence. Our family, friends, community, or even the media often unknowingly perpetuate stereotypes, but these stereotypes often lead to unfair discrimination and persecution when the stereotype is unfavorable. Schoem in this research argued that stereotypes substitute for substantive human understanding and are indicative of the deep chasms of social difference and separation across racial and ethnic differences.

Many researchers in sociology consider 'labeling' as a metaphor to distinguish or identify things and groups of people (Becker, 1963), thereby discriminating and stereotyping people being labeled. This characterization based on assumptions, personal or social opinions, religious perspectives, isolated behaviors, or on any other unfounded evidence can be very harmful and damaging to the person or group, and in respect to this research, even community agencies. Becker (1963) believed that the source of many labeling problems is rooted in social beliefs, which are then used to compare different groups. Becker stipulated that these social norms are then forced upon the minority group or individual, which in turn causes the development of unwanted behaviors.

The labeling of a group or individual then reinforces stereotypes (Ewen & Ewen, 2006). Ewen and Ewen (2006) described stereotyping as a "fixed, commonly held notion or image of a person or group, based on an oversimplification of some observed or imagined trait of behavior or appearance." (p. 27). Similar to labeling, stereotypes reflect the ideas that one group of people hold about a different group of people, but are more synonymous with prejudice and racism because it creates a one-dimensional and often degrading viewpoint of the different group, which then robs them of their humanity (Ewen & Ewen, 2006). Stereotypes evoke images and ideas that are recognized and understood by the group or individual that shares the same views of the minority group that is being labeled. Jacobs (1999) asserted that the marketing campaigns of today's products, music, food, and services help fuel the stereotypes and generalization of groups of people.

Sowell (2005) argued that the stereotyping and labeling of groups creates handicaps, noting that under-represented, labeled groups often mimic these stereotypes out of acceptance by the common belief of their community. These labeled groups may start to use the negative stereotypes as excuses for why they are unable to achieve their goals. These groups may see their future as hopeless because the stereotypes that they are labeled with often result in negative outcomes (Sowell, 2005). Adams, Bell, and Griffin (2007) argued that the majority of the groups that are stereotyped have bought into these labels by absorbing the self-defeating stereotypes imposed upon them by historical events, such as slavery and segregation, media exploitation, and their own community. In summary, these same social stereotypes can also influence the way an agency is viewed by its community and negatively affect the agency's ability to operate.

Concept and Connotations of 'Ghetto'

According to Vergara (1995), the word 'ghetto,' for most Americans, has a different meaning and image from that used to describe the Warsaw ghetto, an earlier sense of the word. In America, the word is used to describe poverty-stricken communities; a section of a city where a subgroup of low-income people resides (Vergara, 1995). These subgroups living in inner-city enclaves are often minority families who are forced to live in these poor conditions because of economic or legal challenges, or social pressures (Hilfiker, 2002). Some of these subgroups may also be receiving government aid to supplement their income, such as welfare, food stamps, Medicaid, and public housing (Hilfiker, 2002). Minority groups living in the ghetto are also considered to be marginalized and oppressed because of the poor quality of life in these areas.

Data reported by the 2000 Census showed that African Americans only made up 12% of the poor in America, and less than half of that 12% live in ghettos. In fact, more white Americans receive welfare support than African Americans, but our society thinks otherwise (Hilfiker, 2002). According to Hilfiker (2002), these stereotypes of ghetto residents invoke images of dangerous-looking black men hanging out on every street corner, uneducated and uncultured families and children, streets infested with gang activity, drug dealers, addicts, and pregnant teens. From our research and professional experience, these stereotypes that have been plaguing African Americans for decades have now attached their stigma onto these urban community centers that serve residents living in the ghetto. The labeling of these community centers as being 'ghetto' invokes mixed feelings by residents, clients, and the employees and administrators of these agencies.

Hudson (2008) distinguished two types of stigma from which an organization can suffer: event-stigma and core-stigma. Event-stigma is attached to a particular circumstance involving an organization, and is normally easy to address and overcome. Core-stigma, on the other hand, indicates a core attribute of the organization is stigmatized. Under Hudson's theory, the community organizations suffer from core-stigmatization, that is, stigmatization because of the negative stereotyping of one or more core attributes of the organization. In this case, the core attributes causing the stigmatization of the organizations are the employees and the clientele they serve.

Method

Community centers, also known as community agencies, are non-profit organizations that offer community assistance through human service support. The services offered by these agencies target low-income and at-risk families and youth. The programs and services foster independence and empowerment. All of these agencies experience high employee turnover; every year they experience decrease in funding and resource limitations, but the service needs of the community keep increasing.

The Rahim and Burrell 2010 study examined four community agencies on the Southwest side of Syracuse, New York, each located 4 to 6 miles apart from each other. The majority of the people living in this area are African Americans and Latino-Americans. All four of these agencies have been categorized and labeled as 'ghetto' agencies, as identified by internal and external sources. These sources claim the following behaviors were observed or experienced while attending a program at these centers or as an employee: rude and unprofessional conduct between employees with clients and each other; unprofessional clothing by employees (perception by source); foul language being used by employees in front of clients or employees not confronting clients (young children) using inappropriate language; the quality of service given to clients; consistency with service providers showing up late for appointments with clients, not prepared and not professionally dressed for the environment, and the lack of structure within programming, documentation, and organization. Data in all four of these agencies serve residents living in the Southwest community. Action research methods were used as tools to provide insights into the nature of these challenges.

Action research as defined in this project consisted of a balance between three key elements: research, participation, and action (Greenwood & Levin, 1998; Herr & Anderson, 2005).

The participation of organizational stakeholders in the inquiry and solution development process required stakeholders to take responsibility for the future and the outcomes that result (Greenwood & Levin, 1998; Herr & Anderson, 2005). The research team in this study had two primary interconnected and interrelated objectives. First, the research team wanted to facilitate participation and elicit discussion among the organizational stakeholders. Specifically, the research team's research goals were:

1. Explore the nature and causes of the negative perceptions and labels of being 'ghetto.'

2. To develop practice-oriented solutions to improve the behaviors and perceptions of the organizations.

Along with the action research framework, qualitative focus group research methods were used because the research team wanted to collect rich descriptive data concerning perceptions of the organizational community members in the context of their everyday organization. The use of focus groups also fit with the use of action research because stakeholders participated in developing their own strategies and solutions (Greenwood & Levin, 1998). In the Rahim and Burrell 2010 study, subjects were separated into four separate groups, with 44 total participants that included employees, managers, and clients (11 total in each category). The groups included 22 women and 22 men. The demographics of the focus groups were 30 African-Americans, 10 Latino-Americans, four Caucasian-Americans. The focus group sessions for each group were conducted on separate occasions to identify consistent viable themes.

Validity

Validity is an important concern for qualitative research and the considerations of validity were used as tools to strengthen the nature of this research study. Several activities were used to test and validate the data. These steps included:

1. Triangulation

2. Checking for alternative explanations and negative evidence.

3. Discussing findings with other experienced researchers and subject matter experts.

4. Comparing developing findings with existing and established theory

5. The use of outside group observers to ensure that feedback response data was recorded, coded, and interpreted accurately. (Creswell, 1994; Maxwell, 2005)

Results

All participants in this study acknowledged the existence of the 'ghetto' labeling issue for their agency and the problems the perception caused to their reputation and to the quality of their programs and services; however, agency stakeholders attempted to pass the blame to actions of others outside their group. For example, managers blamed employees, employees blamed clients, and clients blamed both managers and employees. All participants consistently outlined themes that were contributing factors to negative perceptions and labeling:

1. Poor communication processes between all parties.

2. Poor training on the value and importance of customer service.

3. High employee turnover, which hurt the ability to provide consistent service from trained employees.

4. Low job satisfaction due to the low pay and stressful nature of the work.

5. An absence of the ability to see things from perspectives others.

6. An absence of sense of community and partnership between clients, employees, and supervisors as a collaborative collective group.

7. An absence of awareness of how their actions and behaviors influenced the feelings and perceptions of others.

The collective perspective of the participants were employee behavior and image could be improved by having customer service training, changing their recruitment approaches, clearly outlining employee expectations, mentoring employees, providing consistent feedback on performance, inviting clients to monthly meetings, and professional development training within their organizations. Agency staff and management also concurred that external influences are harder to manage. Given limitations such as caps on salaries and benefit options within their organizations, the managers of the agencies in this study suggested redeveloping career-advancement opportunities to compensate for limited financial resources, a change that in turn would alter their recruitment approaches.

One key perspective that came from the focus groups was that senior managers recognized their limited power to mandate real organizational change. From hearing the feedback from staff, management began to acknowledge that a more effective leadership role for them would be to focus on creating a climate for change, then spreading the lessons of both successes and failures. Feedback from staff supported the concept that management should focus on creating a mission, vision, and general direction in which the agency should move without insisting on the specific solutions which fits well with concepts in the literature that outline the importance of communication and collaboration between management and staff to gain stakeholder support and acceptance (Bennis, 1992).

According to Chabotar (2006), gaining employees' buy-in and acceptance to new strategies, approaches, and change is a critical aspect of getting employees to change a culture of poor perceptions of service and image. One key approach for positive change is to use a bottom-up leadership approach to policy planning via town hall meetings, online surveys, and focus groups to gain insight from staff and stakeholders at all levels (Chabotar, 2006). Consistent and frequent managerial communication and solicitation of feedback from allow stakeholders allows the organization to tap into the collective repository of knowledge by engaging the expertise and experience organizational employees, management, community sponsors, and clients. Open and transparent communications is also required to gain buy-in.

According to Bennis (1992), a successful democratic organizational culture is built by the collective actions, values, and beliefs of all of its citizens. The goal of senior leadership should be clearing out the roadblocks and barriers that hinder employees from doing the appropriate and needed actions and activities (Bennis 1992). This includes removing bureaucratic barriers that have been established even if they were originally established in the best interest of the organization. The positive transformation of an organization can only be achieved through the collective change, growth, and knowledge sharing among members of the group (McGrath, Arrow, & Berdahl, 2000).

Conclusions

Goffman (1959) termed appropriate identities that individuals adopt for their societies as a "front" (p. 22). Consistency of the front is paramount in order to maintain its viability as a believable identity. Goffman's theory provides an important framework for this agency study because it suggests that the behaviors implicated the labeling of organizations and individuals as "ghetto" are deeply engrained, and will be difficult to alter. According to Goffman (1959, 1963), individuals attempt to perform an idealized version of the front, more consistent with the societal perception of the identity when around an audience than when not performing. The idealized version of the front is largely determined by the hegemony of prevailing dominant norms, which also provides the pressure for individuals to conform to that front. Goffman's theories of self-management and development reinforce the results of this study in that the "ghetto" stigma associated with those who use or work at the community agencies may reinforce the stereotype in their attempts to avoid or counteract its negative connotations.

Hudson (2008) outlined that normalizing behaviors could counter stigmatization. This requires that the management acknowledge and reward professional behavior in awards, acknowledgments, and performance reviews. The results of the interviews in this study indicated that all stakeholders need to collaborate, communicate, and function in form of shared organizational mission stewardship and governance because all parties are deeply committed to helping the community and community development.

Kurt Lewin (1958) was one of the preeminent researchers in organizational change theory, positing a three-step method for change: unfreeze, change, and freeze (See Figure 3). According to Lewin, organizational change requires the replacement of old attitudes and behaviors with new ones. The unfreezing step of the process refers to a time of self-reflection among the members of the organization and motivation to prepare the members for the next step. Defense mechanisms and old routines need to be bypassed, and expectations are broken.

Figure 3. Kurt Lewin's Three-Step Process.

The moving step of Lewin (1958) change theory requires a period of cognitive restructuring, in which the members of the organization are provided with information showing that change is possible and desirable. The freezing step refers to a period of returning to the previous comfort levels of the organization, with new goals and expectations formed in the organization's members' minds. This three-step theory to change is particularly applicable to the community agencies of this study because they definitely suffered from inertia, were saddled with excessive work, had undertrained and under-motivated staff, and had limited budgets. The Lewin model offers a way to counteract that inertia.

The work of Cooley (1902), Mead (1934, 1938), and Goffman indicated that individuals' identities were products of interaction and communication with the society around them. The "front" suggested by Goffman can be understood as the labeled stereotype of "ghetto," and it is important to recognize that it is a monumental task to restructure the behavior routines of individuals. Employees interviewed in this study noted that they wanted more effort from the directors to provide them with a professional work environment. New strategies that are geared towards significant change to the environment in these agencies could benefit from management fostering the completion of three-step method forwarded by Lewin (1958). Such an attempted change would require the restructuring of the mindsets of the directors as well.

However, this approach only addresses one of the two core-stigmas attached to the community agencies. The clients of the organization constitute the second core-stigma, and it is unlikely that the organizations will be able to change the stereotypes of the general public. In situations where an unqualified employee group is contributing directly to the labeling problem because of their insecurities or lack of education and experience of other cultures, the onus is on management to use performance management and employee development processes to appropriately develop a system that promotes an environment embracing the opposite qualities. These community agencies can promote fairness and equality by hiring people who normally would not have been hired, and in doing so, they should implement a program that actively fosters workplace professionalism.

The feedback gained from this study stress the importance for organizations to analyze where they may be going wrong and how they can introduce sustainable measures for improvement. This useful organizational analysis can be achieved through the unfreezing step of Lewin's theory of change. Only through such re-evaluation can the inertia of the organization under a stigmatization of 'ghetto' be broken. Bagley (2003) maintains that to uphold an ethical standard, organizations must first understand the law and articulate corporate values. According to Schwartz and Weber (2006), an organization must first develop an "honest assessment of its problems," (p.89) accept understand these problems and formulate a change-management plan that may require modifying the company's organizational and managerial policies and processes. Both the policies and the bylaws of an organization may require adjustments to allow changes to occur regarding intolerance for deleterious behaviors.

REFERENCES

Altman, I., & Taylor, D. (1973). *Social penetration: The development of interpersonal relationships.* New York, NY: Holt, Rinehart, & Winston.

Baldwin, M. (1997). 'Working together reason, learning together: co-operative inquiry in the development of complex practice by teams of social workers', in Reason, P. H. Bradbury, (Ed.), *Handbook of action research: Participative inquiry & practice* (pp. 287–293). Thousand Oaks, CA: Sage Publication Inc.

Becker, H. (1963). *Outsiders: studies in sociology of deviance.* New York, NY: The Free Press.

Bennis, W. (1992, April). *The art-form of leadership, training, and development.* New York, NY: HarperBusiness.

Capra, F. (2003). *The hidden connections,* London, UK: Flamingo.

Chabotar, K. (2006). *Strategic finance: Planning and budgeting for boards, chief executives, and finance officers.* Washington, DC: Association of Governing Boards of Universities and Colleges.

Cheetham, N. (2002). Community participation: What is it? *Transitions, 14*(3): 4.

Cooley, C. (1902; 1922). *Human nature and the social order.* (rev. ed.). New York, NY: Charles Scribner's Sons.

Cooley, C. (1998). *On self and social organization* (rev. ed.). Chicago, IL: University of Chicago Press.

Creswell, J. W. (1994). *Research design: Qualitative & quantitative approaches.* Thousand Oaks, CA: Sage Publications.

Edwards, A. D., & Jones, D. G. (1976). Community and community development. In E. Ntini (Ed.), *The participation of rural based teachers in community development activities.* Chivi district masvingo Zimbabwe, South Africa: South Africa University.

Ewen E., & Ewen M. (2006). *Typecasting. On the arts and sciences of human inequality.* New York, NY: Seven Stories Press.

French, W., & Bell, C. (1979). *Organizational development.* Uppers Saddle River, NJ: Prentice Hall.

Ginzberg, E., Berliner, H., & Ostow, M. (1988). *Young people at risk: Is prevention possible?* Boulder, CO: Westview Press.

Goffman, E. (1959). *The presentation of self in everyday life.* Garden City, NY: Doubleday.

Goffman, E. (1963). *Stigma.* Englewood Cliffs, NJ: Prentice-Hall.

Greenwood, D., & Levin, M. (1998). *Introduction to action research: Social research for social change.* Thousand Oaks, CA: Sage Publications.

Hakanson, J. W. (1981). Community development: who benefits In E. Ntini (Ed.), *The participation of rural based teachers in community development activities.* Chivi district masvingo Zimbabwe, South Africa: South Africa University.

Herr, K., & Andersen, G. L. (2005). *The action research dissertation: A guide for students and faculty.* Thousand Oaks: Wadsworth Publishing.

Hilfiker, D. (2002). *Urban injustice: How ghetto happens.* New York, NY: Seven Stories Press.

Hudson, B. A. (2008). Against all odds: A consideration of core-stigmatized organizations. *Academy of Management Review, 33*(1), 252–266.

Hudson, B. A., & Okhuysen, G. A. (2003). *They're doing what in there? The prevention of social stigma and illegitimacy in the bathhouse.* Paper presented at the annual meeting of the Academy of Management, Seattle.

Irwin, J. (1984). *The jail: managing the underclass in American society.* Berkeley, CA: University of California Press.

Jacobs, B. (1999; 2006). *Race manners for the 21St century.* New York, NY: Harper Collins Publishing, Inc.

Joas, H. (1985). *G. H. Mead: A contemporary re-examination of his thought.* Boston, MA: MIT Press.

Rahim, E. (2010). An application of change management for confronting organizational stigmatization. *Journal of Business & Leadership, 6*(1), 25–37.

About the Authors

Dr. Emad Rahim is an award winning author, educator, entrepreneur and civic leader. Emad holds the following accredited degrees; an AACSB Post-Doctoral Diploma in Marketing and Management Research from Tulane University, Doctorate of Management and Master of Science in Project Management from Colorado Tech's Institute for Advance Studies, and a Bachelor of Science from SUNY Empire State College. He is also a Certified Manager (CM), Project Manager (PMP) and earned an Executive Leadership Certificate from Cornell University and MIT.

Dr. Rahim is a strong advocate for servant leadership. He serves on the Board of Directors for several organizations and volunteers heavily in his community to promote diversity and inclusion. Emad is the Chief Learning Officer at Global i354 LLC and is a university professor on faculty with Morrisville State College, Walden University, Kaplan University, Colorado Tech, Northcentral University, and Syracuse University.

Dr. Rahim serves as a Beyster Scholar for the Beyster Institute, Cohort Chair for the Institute for Advance Studies in Colorado Springs, Professor-in-Residence for the Syracuse Sandbox Project and Technology Garden, and serves on several dissertation and thesis committees.

Dr. Rahim is also an active member of PMI, ICPM, Intellectbase International Consortium and Leadership Greater Syracuse.

To reach Dr. Emad Rahim for information on diversity management, project management or workforce development, please visit his website: www.globali365.com or e-mail: emad.rahim@globali365.com

Dr. Darrell Norman Burrell, D.H.Ed, EdS, MSHRD, MA, MSM is a Presidential Management Fellow, www.pmf.gov. Dr. Burrell is a faculty member in the Global and Community Health Department at George Mason University, Fairfax, VA. Dr. Burrell teaches at Virginia International University. He also teaches in the Doctor of Health Sciences at A.T. Still University in Mesa, AZ.

He teaches as an adjunct in the on-line 'Green' MBA in Sustainability Development at Marylhurst University. He received a doctoral degree in Health Education in Environmental Public Health from A.T. Still University. He has an EdS (Post Master's Terminal Degree) in Higher Education Administration from The George Washington University in Washington, DC. He has graduate degrees in Human Resources Management/Development and Organizational Management from National Louis University and a graduate degree in Sales and Marketing Management from Prescott College. He has over 18 years of management in academia, government, and health care.

He has over 11 years of college teaching experience. Dr. Burrell has over 50 publications and over 30 peer reviewed conference presentations. He has been an academic reviewer for International Journal of Social Health Information Management (IJSHIM), State and Local Government Review, The International Journal of Knowledge, Culture and Change Management, Contemporary Issues in Criminology and the Social Sciences, and Journal of Knowledge & Human Resource Management.

Dr. Darrell Norman Burrell can be reached at: dburrell@atsu.edu or dnburrell@excite.com

CHAPTER 6

The Consumer Learner:
Shifts in the Teacher Student Relationship
Student as Customer

Dr. Gillian Silver and Dr. Cheryl A. Lentz

Throughout the past two decades, the rise of the adult learning model and has removed educational access barriers and enabled more individuals from diverse backgrounds—including women, minorities, full-time employees, and students returning to complete unfinished degrees. This multi-faceted transformation of the post-secondary environment has provided myriad opportunities for those balancing the demands of family, work and community to experience intellectual growth and program achievement. Subsequently, certain variables have led to a cultural shift from a literature and conceptually centric focus to one in which students are becoming *consumer learners*. This chapter addresses, in part, the emergence of the nontraditional adult learner, and the notion of students as drivers of education. The larger work, *Emerging Expectations of a Customer Service Mentality in Post-Secondary Education* upon which this chapter is based explores in-depth how there has been a shift from mastery of the classics to the practicality of action research and faculty coaching as a legitimate process of intellectual development. This component of the discussion best emulates the theme of the refractive thinker series, where this view of learners consuming knowledge and the *product* education symbolizes the diverse views of the adult education community and the process of seeking, evaluating, applying, and challenging knowledge.

The purpose in presenting this content is to offer three unique perspectives—or vantage points—from which to consider the complex requirements of learners, the institutional demands for efficiency and cost-recovery, and the practice obligations of professional educators. Care has been taken to explore the environment in which educators find themselves as a result of both teaching and student experiences. The intention has been to initiate an evolving dialogue—but to do so with balance and fairness, rather than prejudice or from the sensibilities of only one of the three partners involved in the institution-student-educator partnership.

For the purposes of this volume, the multiple lenses are used to create a holistic depiction of some aspects of the evolution of higher education, and to offer excerpts from the larger review of key aspects of the transformation. Clearly all entities and individuals affiliated through the process of adult learning—the institutional administration, the faculty, and the student—bring valuable, and yet often incongruent, dimensions to this discussion.

Readers are invited to join in the contemplative review of these open-ended perspectives for consideration by our colleagues within institutions of higher education and learning. The desire is to understand what these factors, observations, and experiences mean to those facilitating adult learning.

The notion of educational consumption is intriguing to ponder, particularly in the current-day environment of flux. No one would challenge the level of fluidity successfully modeled by the nation's institutions of higher learning in the past two decades. Adaptations include the progression on most campuses, from the traditional 16-week delivery cycle to compressed schedules consisting of 8-week, 6-week, and 5-week classes. This includes the movement from twice-weekly meetings to three or four-hours once a week, and from on-ground and in-person classes to the introduction of distance education sessions to include the online modality.

Colleges and university sites have heeded the call of state regulators and Wall Street (for-profit models) as the demand for demonstrated performance has intensified. Public post-secondary systems were directly challenged to up the ante as new private institutions efficiently entered (and some say) took command of the market. Curriculum content was modified to place greater emphasis on immediately transferable skills. Subsequently, focusing on theoretical and conceptual foundations became a secondary concern.

The sheer impact of nontraditional students (older, re-careering, or returning-to-college learners) meant that most individuals were concurrently working while going to school. Many experienced tremendous time poverty as they were both accountable for young families and, frequently, attending to the needs of aging parents. Degree or certificate attainment became one of many simultaneous demands on the adult student as they juggled a strenuous schedule and increased financial pressures. Subsequently, the demand of the academic process became longer, even with intensified and compressed delivery systems.

The adult learner is now faced with the transactional business approach with truly measurable outcomes, instead of theoretical constructs at its core. The concentration is on relatable ideas with immediately applicable discoveries that can be transferred into professional settings, rather than intellectual conclusions enjoyed merely for the joy of learning. In light of these changes, how will the success of knowledge acquisition be measured? Philosophical and intellectual discourse has given way to the practical *what have you done for me lately* approach. Students now evaluate curriculum, programs and faculty from the position of utility. Information must provide function, and serve an end purpose beyond content mastery.

While the reconfigurations and institutional resiliency served as a testament to the ability to respond proficiently, new challenges began to emerge. A willingness to evolve is only one dimension of the necessary adjustments. Secondary educators have begun reporting that students are exhibiting new behavioral dimensions. Attention spans seemed shorter in exhausted adults. Resistance to information reviewed as non-essential was voiced boldly without hesitation. Students demanded to know *why* content was relevant, and often reject the establishment of a theoretical base as they are anxious for direct conclusions. Post-secondary educators face a distinctive quagmire, how to both please student demands for transferrable experience and ensure that the integrity of the process is not compromised in the process.

Increasingly, students want concrete direct answers handed to them. Case studies and other forms of practical inquiry requiring personal analysis and interpretation are now preferred delivery methods. The faculty members are being pressed to make adjustments that ensured every element of the learning experience is relevant, but some have suggested these modifications come with a concerning compromise. Heidelberg (2008) documented the convergence of an *edutainment* movement where there is less use for the classical professoriate model and a *blended delivery zone* of entertainment and education. Students, challenged by massive amounts of preparation (reading individual and group assignments), may now seek amusement when convened for class.

Adult learners desire technology-based delivery methods:

stylishly designed PowerPoints, real-time Internet searches, videos, and forays into You-Tube postings. Rather quickly, the demand for digestible education that could be *consumed* by learners has become an eye-opening call for action. Educators may lament the loss of substance and the potential sacrifice of content as complex ideas are frequently broken down to the most common denominator to heighten learner appeal.

Administrators speak to the requirements of external accrediting bodies to validate degree programs and the necessity of an outcome-based approach. The business community now meets with administrators to request more accessible tuition rates and more industry-specific material. Although the concurrently emerging shifts in focus are both pronounced and multi-faceted, perhaps the largest philosophical transformation of all is creeping into view. The higher education area was evolving into a provider (italics) with a business market transaction mentality. The result of this transformation: a student-as-customer disposition.

Has the mindset among learners emerged from the application of a business model to the *consumer* of education? Is this change a reflection of a stressed-out populace surviving in an increasingly complex, competitive society in which the Americans brain-trust no longer prevailed? Are reduced attention spans and boredom serving as contributing elements? An absence in the mainstream literature exits to postulate on the most dominant reason, but experiential associations abound.

Demographic and psychographic indicators point to an aging society, with the largest amount of population growth occurring in the United States being recorded in the states west of the Mississippi in the lower 48: Arizona, Nevada, California, Utah, Colorado, and Washington (Case & Alward, 1997; U.S. Census, 2010). As individuals recognizing time is finite, expectations are altered. Further, post-secondary institutions in these geographic areas must adapt to the life-long learning expectations and service requirements of these older students.

The dramatic effects of a period of corporate compression, (middle-management downsizing), creation of multi-national conglomerates, and followed by arguably the greatest economic downturn since the Depression, means that stable, well-compensated positions with benefits were suddenly a hot commodity. Employers under the guide of efficiency management have been leveraging the opportunities to eliminate full-time jobs. Part-time, on-call, temporary duty roles are becoming the norm.

Rationalizing these conclusions could be accepted by administrators, faculty, and students alike, but it seems the resulting classroom conduct modifications are symbolizing an even greater shift. Relationships among the three collaborative partners are being challenged by a question of whether empowered 'buyers' of education—these new consumers—will achieve academic standards or challenge their veracity.

Vantage point #1: Administrators

Education is about the pursuit of knowledge, but increasingly institutions must operate with a return on investment focus. This *transactional business* approach was emerging concurrently as education lost its value as a mission to educate as a mechanism for knowledge transfer. Instead, the process of educational delivery is emerging as a true business model with a profit-driven focus. With budgets being slashed, sustainability and survivability of the academic institutions is being challenged. Can post-secondary institutions survive with current models? Or will they fail the test of adaptation? Has the goal for education evolved from classroom learning objectives to coaching to profit driven results and efficiency? Or, is the overarching directive in times of funding pressure shifting to achievement of economies of scale?

Administrators are, therefore, charged with two concurrent demands. These demands are to ensure the institutional mission by building an educated populace to support industry, as well as to produce profitable programs that emulate lean management principles and tight cost control.

Student choice in the marketplace, is this a competitive advantage? For-profit institutions are taking to the airwaves of TV, radio, and social media to advertise and compete for tuition dollars. In the process of building institutional branding and program visibility, has education become commercialized? Instead of underscoring the importance of college at the high school level via the traditional academic pathways of guidance counselors and administrators, post-secondary institutions are using a consumer-centric marketing focus similar to the mass media channels used to advertise new homes for sales or invest-ment opportunities. Has the heated marketing to generate tuition dollars raised the competitive bar to a new level? Is this a wise approach? Should the concentration be on reaching desirable numbers in the classroom versus recruiting appropriately quali-fied prospective students as future minds to educate?

Vantage point #2: Faculty

Educators are caught in a bizarre conundrum and being pulled simultaneously by both administrators and students. Many fac-ulty members are starting to question if struggling institutions, driven by a profit motive are acquiescing to this incentive to please as a means to retain students not as adult learners but as income. Concurrently, faculty report the emerging demand by students is much like a business exchange. Students desire a level of entertainment in their contact hours, which evolves the professor into a customer service agent. Students expect to like their faculty, to be pleased by their faculty, and to demand customer satisfaction of their investment of tuition dollars much in the way one would buy a hamburger or a sports car. Adult learners insist upon a quality experience. Education has been reduced to a business *transaction* instead of an intellectual exchange of scholarly premise or theory discussion.

As part of a faculty's evaluation, instead of how well a faculty presents materials in the classroom, achieves or exceeds learning outcomes measured by student achievement or attainment, there is an additional element of popularity among the learners. This shift from viewing the educator as a contact expert to the educator as a faculty (or not) translates into a factor of whether a faculty has met all of a student's social expectations as part of the educational experience. Further, the administration takes these satisfaction scores into consideration when offering future contracts. This is of particular interest to part time or adjunct faculty, who report enhanced pressure to satisfy learners' interpersonal preferences and sense of what level of work, is *manageable,* rather than *challenging.*

Somewhere in this process, the educator has been asked to meet a customer service and social expectation in the mind of the student. The professor is no longer revered for their depth of scholarly knowledge and andragogical skill. Instead, the educator is now at the subjective mercy of a popularity contest as to how well they pleased the personal and entertainment expectations of their students, as opposed to learning objectives, curriculum agendas, and demonstration of learned course skills and theory. This begs the question, when did this paradigm shift from educator to customer service agent occur exactly? Is this a positive or natural direction for this relationship to evolve?

As the academic institute's representatives with *their feet on the ground,* faculty offers the most identifiable touch point in the student experience. Clearly, faculty provide the bulk of the direct educational exchange through interpretation of the essential core competencies to be gained in the course, delivery of the salient ideas and assignment instructions, and assessment of learner outcomes. Interpersonally, the educator's disposition shapes the student's view of the subject matter and its complexity. The professor holds within his or her classroom management strategies the ability to foster dynamic dialogue or to make potentially compelling content invigorating and pertinent, rather than flat, and nontransferable. In an emerging *consumer learner* environment, the faculty member can engage and direct understanding. They can reinforce the choice of the institution as a good fit, and can demonstrate how diligently student interests are supported. By placing continual emphasis on quality, post-secondary educators can provide a base of knowledge that is compelling, attractive, and pertinent.

Vantage point #3: Students

The student views the faculty/student relationship as one of a transactional exchange. This perspective suggests inquiry; has the student received an adequate return on their investment (ROI) in terms of time, financial investment, social experience and relevance? Adult learners who might otherwise have seen the educational process as vital, stimulating and life-altering suddenly had become pragmatic. College had a price—a steep one at that—time, energy, and challenging tuition and fees. In a free-enterprise system of many options a natural outgrowth was the view that money was exchanged—rather than invested—in an educational product. The process, the personal evolution the individual had the capacity to experience was subservient to the end goal: a formal piece of paper documenting degree completion.

Contemporary students look to the process of obtaining this degree as one of social compliance. Has the professor met their entertainment goals? Has the professor become the personal and charming face of education as a spokesperson might be rated? When did the social experience circumvent or subjugate the higher purpose of learning? Since when does a student's personal like of a professor instead of respect take more of a focal point and center stage of prominence in the mind of the adult learner? Where is the correlation of likability to andragogical skill? Is it necessary that a student like his or her educator to learn effectively from them? Is this customer service focus replacing the need for scholars in the classroom?

As the cost of a college education escalates, students and parents alike are weighing the merits of a multiple-year investment that may generate a $35,000 (Baccalaureate) to six-figure (Masters) debt (The College Board Policy Center, 2011), the economics of higher education, and the often complex nature of loan structures, makes the decision to pursue a degree increasingly complex. Coupled with the recession and extensive level of job compression that continues to be experienced by the nation, students are evaluating the opportunities of college against the financial return of acquiring a degree and, ideally, the acquisition of a higher compensated position following graduation. This question of value doesn't dissipate once enrolled. Learners continue to weigh their interest in the subject matter, their ability to succeed, and the overall opinion of the educational experience against the expense.

For some, the notion of the *consumer learner* is concentrated here—on the cost of education. Some students conclude they are engaged in a purchase, and adopt an expectation that course-work will be limited and easy to complete, and satisfaction is guaranteed. This vantage point frequently contradicts the administrative position that education involves rigor. The prevailing faculty view that there is a natural variance in learner performance and that a grade of an 'A' is earned, not awarded or up for negotiation.

Summary

When external variables such as stable employment and professional advancement appear compromised, it becomes necessary to view post-secondary education from the perspective of a consumer mentality. The return on investment (ROI quotient) must be persuasive for the adult learner to make the commitment to a degree program. Student must have confidence in the curriculum and the instruction and view the experience as meritorious in light of the complex purchase decision. This chapter encompassed the transformational dispositions toward education. Of all of the ideas expressed, the most crucial to consider is that educational integrity must not be compromised even when powerful market pressures favor the consumer. Students must accept that rigor and assessment of achievement are large components of the journey toward knowledge acquisition and crucial to leverage if that knowledge is to be applicable in life and in work.

As a result of this examination of numerous internal and external variables impacting the nature of adult learning, we contend that the environment of post-secondary education has indeed changed. The context has been slowly adapted from one of a foundational theoretical quest for knowledge to a business transactional exchange where the consumer learner is at the forefront. In the process, the role of the educator, the administrator and the student has also experienced significant transition. Of particular note is the student's obligation to recognize their intellectual and professional transfer needs that require clarity. A faculty can 'take a proverbial horse to water,' yet even though they cannot be made to drink, students can, potentially, be encouraged to feel the *thirst*.

To read more on the evolution of the consumer learner and its impact, go to info@consumerlearner.com. Emerging Expectations of a Customer Service Mentality in Post-Secondary Education (italics please, no underline) by Dr. Gillian Silver and Dr. Cheryl Lentz will be published in winter 2011 by Pensiero Press.

REFERENCES

Case, P., & Alward, G. (1997). *Patterns of demographic, economic and value change in the Western United States*. A report to the Western Water Policy Review Advisory Commission.

Heidelberg, C. A. I. (2008). *Edutainment and convergence: Utilization in higher education from the perspective of entertainment professionals*. (Doctoral dissertation). Retrieved from *ProQuest Dissertations and Theses database* http://search.proquest.com/docview/89202555?accountid=35812

The College Board Policy Center. (2011). Retrieved from http://advocacy.collegeboard.org/

The U.S. Census. (2010). Retrieved from http://2010.census.gov/2010census/

About the Authors

Dr. Gillian Silver is an accomplished integrated marketing communications and strategic planning professional. Her experience spans corporate-level positions for companies with domestic and international operations. She has nearly two decades in the higher education arena preparing Bachelor's, Master's and Doctorate level students. Dr. Gillian's student-oriented philosophy has earned her numerous awards from multiple institutions.

She holds the Accredited Business Communicator designation from IABC, and was named IABC's "Communicator of the Year," and NAWBO's "Woman of the Year/Marketing." Dr. Gillian was twice recognized with the "Women of Excellence/Faculty Award" by the College of Southern Nevada. The institution also selected her for the "President's Service Award," and she received the Mediators of Southern Nevada's "Peacemaker's Award."

Dr. Gillian achieved a Ph.D. in Organizational Leadership from the University of Phoenix, School of Advanced Studies, a Master's in Organizational Development (MS) from the University of Phoenix and a both a Bachelor's in Mass Communications/Journalism (BS) and a Bachelor's in Fine Arts (BA) from Stephens College.

Published works include her dissertation: *A Qualitative Examination: Ways of Leading Among Non-Profit Executives,* and the book *The Consumer Learner: Emergence and Expectations of a Customer Service Mentality in Post-Secondary Education* with co-author Dr. Cheryl Lentz.

Please contact Dr. Gillian Silver at gsilver@strategicresource.com

Southern Nevadan internationally published and award winning author, Dr. Cheryl A. Lentz holds several accredited degrees; a Bachelor of Arts (BA) from the University of Illinois, Urbana-Champaign; a Master of Science in International Relations (MSIR) from Troy University; and a Doctorate of Management (DM) in Organizational Leadership from University of Phoenix School of Advanced Studies.

Dr. Cheryl, affectionately known as 'Doc C' to her students, is a university professor on faculty with Colorado State University-Global, Embry-Riddle University, University of Phoenix, The University of the Rockies, and Walden University. Dr. Cheryl serves as a dissertation committee member, faculty mentor, is a dissertation coach, and offers expertise in editing in APA style for graduate thesis and doctoral dissertations. She has earned her Sloan C Certification from Colorado State University– Global as well as her Quality Matters Peer Reviewer (APP/PRC) Certification.

Dr. Cheryl is also an active member of Alpha Sigma Alpha Sorority.

Additional published works include her dissertation: *Strategic Decision Making in Organizational Performance: A Quantitative Study of Employee Inclusiveness, The Golden Palace Theory of Management, Journey Outside the Golden Palace,* Effective *Study Skills in 5 Simple Steps, The Refractive Thinker: Vol. I: An Anthology of Doctoral Learners, Vol. II: Research Methodology, Vol. III. Change Management, Volume IV: Ethics, Leadership, and Globalization,* and *Volume V: Strategy in Innovation.* For additional details, please visit her website: http://www.drcheryllentz .com

To reach Dr. Cheryl Lentz for information on any of these topics, please e-mail: drcheryllentz@gmail.com

CHAPTER 7

A Leaders' Influence on Employee-Students Seeking Post-Secondary Education

Dr. Richard Wolodkowicz

Corporate education initiatives that include tuition reimbursement are a considerable corporate investment. American organizations spend approximately $10 billion annually on tuition assistance programs (Halfond, 2006). According to Olesen (1999), 98% of corporations with 5,000 or more employees offer professional development, and 93% offer educational assistance.

Employees who receive corporate tuition reimbursement and complete a degree tend to leave the organization that sponsored their education (Benson, 2002; Benson, Finegold, & Mohrman, 2004). According to Benson (2002, 2003), there is a significant positive relationship between seeking employer-funded tuition reimbursement and employees' *intention to turnover*. Employees understand that education increases their marketability and Ramsay-Smith (2004) estimated the costs associated with employee turnover at 1 to 2 years' salary of the departing employee, not including the tuition expense. The costs of turnover consisting of lost productivity, lost human capital, decreased morale, and rehiring costs can have a negative effect on corporate profits (Hacker, 2003; Koch, 2006).

Employee-students present an outward sign of intending to

turnover, through their desire to complete a degree seeking education; the cost of that turnover coupled to the expense incurred for the general education is substantial. Unless corporate leaders better manage their investments in the education of employees, they will continue to witness newly educated employees seeking employment elsewhere.

Overview of the Study

The focus of the 2008 Wolodkowicz study was on investigating the importance and impact of specific leadership attributes on employee-students' intention to stay with or leave their current employer. The premise of the study was that specific leadership attributes could decrease both employees' intention to turnover and actual turnover.

The goal was to examine seven leadership attributes in supervisors of employee-students seeking post-secondary educations and determine the predictive value of these attributes with regard to intention to turnover. The leadership attributes examined were (a) authenticity and trustworthiness; (b) change agent; (c) charisma; (d) communication; (e) learner; (f) mentor; and (g) visionary. The leadership qualities selected are characteristics of leadership or traits of leaders and are a subset of all possible leadership qualities. A quantitative research instrument, the Leadership Quality Survey (LQS), was developed as the means to identify employees' intention to turnover and the importance employee-students gave to the leadership attributes. The participants' ranking of leadership attributes provided insight in the factors that influenced the employee-students in the sample regarding their intention to turnover.

There exists little or no evidence of whether leadership attributes in supervisors minimize turnover in employee-students seeking a post-secondary degree. The purpose of the 2008 Wolodkowicz research was to determine the importance of the selected leadership attributes and their effect on intention to stay or leave in the population of full-time employees seeking an advanced degree. A reduction in turnover in employee-students seeking advanced degrees through tuition reimbursement could yield the two immediate organizational benefits of (a) moderating the cost of turnover and (b) increasing human capital.

Understanding the intention to turnover and the influence of leadership attributes is necessary to reduce the costs associated with turnover and ensure that talented employees remain with the organization that funded their education. Logistic regression was used to analyze leadership qualities data collected through the survey; by separating intention to turnover into the dichotomous criterion of stay or leave, logistic regression analysis was used to test two hypotheses and evaluate the seven leadership attributes for their predictive value about employees' intention to stay or leave.

Theory

In the 1960s, Becker (1975) developed the human capital theory in which he posited that an employee's education and learning were instrumental to the production of goods. The human capital theory addressed the knowledge and skills of the human resources of organizations. Becker presented education or training as organizational activities affecting both present and future productivity and explained that any investment in education increased workers' knowledge and productivity. An increase in knowledge and productivity also increased employee wages. Education is a substantial component of human capital theory as employee education is a central element in the theory.

Education

Within the framework of the 2008 Wolodkowicz study, many factors influence the desire to obtain more education. Tuition reimbursement is one factor influencing employee education as employees participating in tuition reimbursement are focused and motivated on completing some accredited transferable knowledge. Booth and Bryan (2005) found that employer-funded education resulting in accreditation was strongly related to higher employee wages with both current and future employers. Boggess and Ryan (2002) evaluated the 1997 economic census data and showed both male and female college graduates averaged about a 30% increase in earnings compared to their high school graduate counterparts. Higher earnings might be the primary motivation of employees for seeking education. According to Loewenstein and Spletzer (1998), employees expected to earn higher wages from increased education and employees seek new employment if their current employer does not meet newly educated employees' expectations for future wages. Education has a direct impact on turnover based on Loewenstein and Spletzer's (1998) study.

Effect of Education on Turnover

Another aspect of the intention to turnover is how turnover is affected by the student-employee education. Researchers have demonstrated that education could lead to an increased intention to turnover as in Benson's (2003) quantitative study finding a significant positive relationship between employees utilizing tuition reimbursement and their intention to turnover. In the human capital theory, Becker (1975) incorporated the belief that companies should not pay to increase employees' general skills because increased skills lead to increased turnover.

Benson et al. (2004) asked the question "Does investing

in employees' marketable skills reduce turnover?" (p. 315). Through an analysis of survey results of 9,439 "employees of a large manufacturer" (p. 315), Benson et al. found employees receiving graduate degrees were 76% more likely to leave the sponsoring firm than employees who did not receive a degree. Hersch (1991) noted there was a statistically significant correlation ($p < 0.01$) between overeducated employees and their tendency to turnover. Although corporate investment in education could reduce employee turnover through increased employee satisfaction with the organization, prevailing data demonstrated that education might lead to increased turnover and an increased intention to turnover.

Employee Turnover

A substantial amount of research was available on employee turnover as the dependent variable with a focus on the costs to organizations of employee turnover and the need to minimize these costs (Glebbeek & Bax, 2004). The literature offered techniques to reduce and manage turnover (Frank, Finnegan, & Taylor, 2004), details on the costs of turnover (Koch, 2006), and discussions of other factors influencing turnover (Bufe & Murphy, 2004), including education (Benson, 2003).

Employee turnover consists of (a) voluntary employee turnover originating with the employee and (b) involuntary turnover initiated by the organization. Voluntary employee turnover resulting from an employee seeking the potential benefit of an education was the central consideration of the 2008 Wolodkowicz study. Other voluntary turnover such as for example employee relocation was excluded.

The choice of employee turnover as dependent variable was appropriate to the 2008 Wolodkowicz study for several reasons. First, the central goal was to consider and understand how various leadership attributes might minimize turnover, specifically turnover influenced by education. Second, education is a factor affecting employee turnover. Third, employee turnover as an associated cost consisting of various elements including tuition reimbursement and the cost of turnover financially affects an organization. Lastly, turnover resulting from education is the core tenet of the human capital theory.

Leadership

A review of leadership and employee retention literature revealed a broad range of discussions including many industries and various leadership approaches. The literature included the nursing (Naude & McCabe, 2005), education (Phelan, 2005), and contracting fields (Miodonski, 2005) and the broad leadership categories of trust, respect, motivation, vision, and concern for staff (Gupta, 2005; Miodonski, 2005; Naude & McCabe, 2005; Phelan, 2005), among the leadership attributes and approaches to improve retention and reduce turnover. No previous studies were found that quantified the impact of specific leadership attributes in managers and leaders to minimize turnover in employees who seek an advanced degree.

Types of Leadership Attributes

Some leadership attributes have been shown to reduce turnover (Garger, 1999; Taylor, 2002), but no information was available focusing on the population of employee-students. In the 2008 Wolodkowicz study, leadership attributes were the independent variable. The focus on several leadership attributes and their influence on employee intention to turnover. When employees are dissatisfied with their work or consider their work unproductive, they tend to turnover. Leadership can affect the variables of satisfaction and productivity, either positively or negatively, and can influence turnover. Taylor (2002) held managers responsible for building an environment leading to employee retention. The 2008 Wolodkowicz study was an investigation of the importance of a set of leadership attributes in leaders to reduce turnover in employees.

While an advanced degree might not directly lead to a better position, the education itself has an effect on the employee, their productivity, satisfaction, and performance. Education increases an employee's desire to look for employment elsewhere. When employees leave their company, the costs to the organization above the cost of tuition include replacement costs, lost productivity, and decreased morale. Organizations too often fail to treat education strategically and more readily focus on the tactical aspects of education (Daniels, 2003).

Method

The goal of the 2008 Wolodkowicz study was to explore the predictive value of seven leadership attributes for employees' intention to stay or leave. Two research questions directed the 2008 Wolodkowicz study. The first question (RQ_1) queried whether demographic variables predicted employees' intention to stay with or leave a company upon completion of their degree. The set of demographic information collected in the survey included (a) age, (b) gender, (c) percent of education reimbursed, (d) length of time with the employer, (e) degree sought, and (f) current country location. These data were measured to determine their predictive value on employees' intention to stay or leave among employee-students. The second question (RQ_2) asked whether the selected leadership attributes predicted employee-student intention to stay with or leave their company upon completion of a post-secondary degree. The seven leadership attributes comprised the independent variable and were measured to determine their effect on employee intention to turnover among employee-students.

Employee intention to turnover as the dependent variable was appropriate because education affects whether employees consider leaving their employer. Employee intention to turnover is often the best forecast for actual turnover (Thatcher, Stepina, & Boyle, 2002; van Breukelen, van der Vlist, & Steensma, 2004). The Leadership Qualities Survey (LQS) was developed to measure and assess whether leadership attributes could predict employees' intention to stay with or leave their employer. The quantitative research design was selected because numerical data are objective, value free, and given to statistical analysis (Neuman, 2003).

The data analysis consisted of various statistical methods including descriptive statistics and logistic regression. A logistic regression test was used to test Hypotheses 1 and 2 and evaluate both the demographic data and seven leadership attributes to determine the best predictors of employee intention to stay or leave. The exploration of the attitudes and opinions of employee-students on intention to turnover provided answers to the research questions.

Two research questions directed the 2008 Wolodkowicz study:

RQ1: To what extent do demographic variables such as age, current country location, degree sought, gender, percent of education funding, or length of time with the company predict employee intention to stay or leave their employer?

RQ2: How does the importance of leadership attributes such as authentic, change agent, charismatic, communicative, learner, mentor, or visionary predict employee intention to stay or leave their employer?

The population was employee-students who pursued a post-secondary education while employed full-time in the financial services industry. Only employees in a degree seeking education program were included as potential participants. Training, whether general or specific, as well as certificate education were excluded from the study (Barrett & O'Connell, 2001; Becker, 1975). Additionally, all employees who used tuition reimbursement, regardless of degree sought, percent of reimbursement, previous education, or duration of tuition reimbursement remaining, were members of the population. Identifying all the members of the population to conduct a survey was not possible for various reasons that included privacy issues regarding personnel data and survey administration to the entire group. A convenience sample totaling 219 respondents with 158 using tuition reimbursement is assumed typical of the population (Salkind, 2003).

The Leadership Qualities Survey (LQS) instrument was designed specifically for the 2008 Wolodkowicz study. A quantitative electronic web survey (Dillman, 2007) was used to measure the degree of importance of each item to the respondents. Items were created to measure the impact of leadership qualities on employee intention to leave or stay. A 5-point scale was selected to obtain a level of granularity greater than a dichotomous scale would offer. The scale used in the research ranged from *very important, somewhat important, important, less important,* and *not important.*

Data Analysis

A logistic regression analysis was used to address the first and second research questions and hypotheses. The analysis highlighted the demographic variables, testing if any demographic successfully predicted an employees' intention to stay with or leave their employer. Based on the results of the analysis, an organization can focus employee retention efforts on a specific demographic in an effort to reduce employee turnover.

Additionally, a logistic regression was also used to test whether any of the seven selected leadership attributes predicted an employees' intention to stay with or leave their employer. Based on the results of the regression analysis and the best predictors of employee intention to stay or leave, an organization can undertake various initiatives and programs to improve the leadership qualities in their management in an effort to improve employee retention.

Findings

A combination of snowball sampling and the agreement of two banks to participate in the research study yielded a total of 219 respondents. Of the 219 respondents, 158 (72.1%) were identified as acquiring their education funded through tuition reimbursement. The 61 respondents who could not be directly identified as using tuition reimbursement were removed from the sample. Full-time employees accounted for 76%, or 120 respondents, and 115 respondents were employed in the financial services industry. The population was expanded to include all respondents whose education was funded through tuition reimbursement to maximize the available data for analysis.

In the sample of 158 respondents who participated in tuition reimbursement, 98 were men (62.0%) and 58 were women (36.7%). The age range was from 23 to 58 years, averaging an age of 32.3 years ($n = 155$) ($SD = 6.2$). The respondents' mean duration with their employer was 5.5 years ($n = 157$) ($SD = 4.2$). The LQS inquired about the type of education the respondents sought with tuition reimbursement. Organizations are funding 127 master's degrees (81.4%), 23 bachelor or associate's degrees (14.7%), and 6 doctorates (3.8%).

INSTRUMENT FACTOR ANALYSIS

The Leadership Qualities Survey (LQS) was designed to measure eight factors including employee intention to turnover and seven leadership qualities. A factor analysis was conducted to examine the validity and reliability of the LQS. The expectation was the items would load on the eight designed factors. However, the factor analysis identified 4 factors; Authenticity, Mentor and Communication, Learner, Charisma-Change Agent-Visionary. In general, all the leadership qualities could be combined and exhibited by any leader. While the items in the factor analysis differ from the original intent, the factor analysis and reliability on the subscales indicate four practical factors with a high level of internal consistency and reliability.

Factor 1: Authenticity

The leadership quality constructs in Factor 1 are most closely aligned with the leadership quality of authenticity. Constructs within authenticity include leaders' ethical behavior, leaders doing what is right, and leaders as role models.

Factor 2: Mentor and Communication

The leadership quality constructs in Factor 2 are most closely aligned with the leadership quality mentor and communication. Constructs within mentor and communication include leaders sharing knowledge, providing feedback, speaking clearly, and motivating followers.

Factor 3: Learner

The leadership quality constructs in Factor 3 are most closely aligned with the single leadership quality learner and consist of seven items. Constructs within learner include leaders' support and encouragement for learning, personal growth, and personal development.

Factor 4: Charisma, Change Agent, and Visionary

The fourth factor is a conglomerate of concepts more difficult to define that includes leaders' dynamism, self-confidence, vision, and influence. The leadership quality constructs in Factor 4 are most closely aligned with the leadership qualities of charisma, change agent, and visionary.

Logistic regressions were calculated to gauge the predictability of employee turnover intention to answer the research questions and to test the hypotheses. Logistic regression models the influence of several predictor variables on a dependent variable and attempts to predict a categorical result in the dependent variable (Worster, Fan, & Ismaila, 2007). Logistic regression in the 2008 Wolodkowicz study predicted whether demographics or leadership variables influenced employee-students to either stay with or leave their employer.

Research Question 1

Six demographic variables were planned for logistic regression analysis to measure predictability of employee intention to stay or leave. The demographic variables collected in the research study included age, current country location, degree sought, gender, percent of tuition reimbursement, and years employed with the company. However, current country location was removed as the responses were heavily weighted on one answer (e.g., 128 respondents from Region 1, the United States). Within the five remaining demographic variables, degree sought was expanded to the six component degrees increasing the total demographic variables to 10 possible predictors for intention to turnover including Gender, Age, Percent of Reimbursement, Years Employed, Associates Degree, Bachelor's Degree, Master's Degree, M.B.A., Executive M.B.A., and Doctorate.

A logistic regression used the 10 demographic variables to gauge how these variables predicted employee intention to turnover. A total of 132 respondents were included in the demographic logistic regression data analysis. The results of the logistic regression analysis with demographic variables show none of the demographic variables were significant predictors of employee-students' intention to stay or leave. Hypothesis $H1_0$ for the first research question was supported because the demographics are not significant predictors of employee-student intention to stay or leave.

Research Question 2

The leadership qualities were used to test the hypothesis associated with the second research question. A total of 136 of the 158 respondents were included in the leadership qualities analysis. Results from seven questions directly testing the seven leadership qualities show none of the attributes are predictive of an employee-student's intention to turnover. Individual leadership attributes are not significant predictors of employee-student intention to stay or leave. Additional analysis related to leadership including the idea of a general lack of leadership and four factors was considered.

Logistic Regression: General Lack of Leadership

In testing the importance of a general lack of leadership as a motivating factor to seek employment elsewhere a total 141 respondents were included in the analysis. The results show a general lack of leadership is a significant predictor of employee-students' intention to stay or leave their employer. The Odds Ratio value of 1.64 indicates that, with each point rise on the general lack of leadership subscale, employee-students are 1.64 times more likely to turnover.

Logistic Regression: Four Factors

A third logistic regression analysis was performed on the responses from 129 respondents to determine employee-student intention to turnover based on four factors identified from the factor analysis. The results show 3 of the 4 factors were not predictive of an employee-student's intention to turnover. However, the learner factor was a statistically significant predictor of employee intention to turnover. The Odds Ratio value or 0.84 indicates that, for every one point increase in value in the scale for learner, an employee-student is .845 times more likely to turnover. Alternatively, the employee-students are more likely to stay with their employer with increases in the scale for learner.

Rank Order Frequencies

Finally, participants were asked to rank order the three most important leadership qualities. First, rankings sought the respondents' opinion on the most important attributes for leaders to possess and demonstrate in their work lives; the results show respondents most valued qualities of authenticity, followed by a communicative leader, visionary leaders, and mentors. Respondents also most valued authenticity, communicative leader, mentors, and change agents in their immediate supervisors.

Summary of Findings

Five demographic variables and seven leadership qualities were examined to answer two research questions and determine whether either demographics or leadership qualities could predict employee-student intention to turnover. A factor analysis concluded that seven leadership qualities in 35 constructs with moderate reliability statistics would have an improved reliability when factor loading into four new factors was accomplished. Intention to turnover was made into a dichotomous variable through a sum of the scores for three research questions and cumulative results split at approximately the 50% point. Logistic regression analysis was selected as the primary statistical method to assess predictability of intention to turnover.

A logistic regression analysis for the demographic variables was conducted. None of the individual demographic variables was a statistically significant predictor for employee intention to stay or leave, resulting in failure to reject $H1_0$. Demographics are not statistically significant predictors of employee intention to turnover.

Three logistic regression analyses were conducted in relation to the second research question. The first logistic regression analysis utilized the seven individual leadership qualities. The direct inquiry to leadership qualities was not statistically significant. None of the seven individual leadership variables was a statistically significant predictor of employee intention to stay or leave, resulting in failure to reject $H2_0$. The seven leadership qualities of authenticity, communication, change agent, charisma, mentor, learner, and visionary are not statistically significant predictors of employee intention to turnover.

Further data analysis included a logistic regression based on the results of a question focused on a general lack of leadership as a possible predictor of employee intention to turnover. In this case, the results from a logistic regression analysis of responses to a general lack of leadership yielded a statistically significant result, $p < .001$. In exploring the frequency data for a general lack of leadership, 68% of the respondents who intended to stay rated general lack of leadership as *not important* or *less important* while nearly half of those intending to leave rated general lack of leadership as *very important* or *somewhat important*.

The final logistic regression analysis was conducted utilizing the four new factors resulting from the factor analysis. While three factors were not statistically significant predictors of employee intention to turnover, the *learner* factor yielded a statistically significant result, $p = .04$. Learner was a significant predictor of employee intention to turnover.

In addition to the logistic regression analyses, respondents were asked to rank order leadership qualities. Respondents were asked to consider the most important leadership qualities for their direct leaders to possess and to consider the leadership qualities the respondents most valued. In both cases, authenticity and communication were the most important qualities, and charisma and learner were least important.

Conclusion

The problem addressed in the 2008 Wolodkowicz study was the effects of leaders on employees' intention to turnover after having used tuition reimbursement to obtain a post-secondary degree. The purpose of the research study was to examine seven leadership attributes in supervisors of employee-students and the predictive value of the leadership attributes with regard to intention to turnover.

Employees understand that education increases their marketability. Employee-students seeking a post-secondary degree also present an outward sign of intending to turnover, through their desire to complete a degree seeking education. Additionally, degree-seeking employee-students are statistically more likely to turnover (Barrett & O'Connell, 2001; Benson, 2002, 2003; McLean, 2005). The costs associated with employee turnover are substantial and have been estimated at 1 to 2 years' salary of the departing employee, not including the actual education expense (Ramsay-Smith, 2004).

Knowledge about the intention to turnover and the influence of leadership attributes can help develop strategies to reduce the costs of turnover and ensure that talented employees remain with the organization funding their education. An organization understanding how to mitigate turnover in employees seeking post-secondary educations can reduce expenses and improve the corporation's profits.

Understanding employee turnover before it happens can be a complex challenge. The responsibilities associated with identifying and reducing turnover are large, but at risk are human capital and the costs associated with turnover. Predicting employee intention to turnover in the group of employee-students utilizing tuition reimbursement produced several conclusions. Individual leadership qualities are not significant predictors of an employee-student's intention to stay or leave. Conversely, the common concept of leadership represented in a *general lack of leadership* is a significant predictor of employee-student intention to turnover. Furthermore, employee-students seeking a post-secondary degree value leaders who are learners and supportive of education and personal development. The learner factor is a significant predictor of employee intention to stay. Finally, demographic data are not predictors of employee-student intention to stay or leave.

Constructs within the learner factor included leaders' support and encouragement for learning, personal growth, and personal development. Employees using tuition reimbursement are learners themselves and based on the finding from the 2008 Wolodkowicz research, this group values a leader who is a learner and is supportive of the employee's learning and growth.

Leaders and managers should ensure they value learning by supporting education and increasing their involvement in employee-students' personal growth and development. Added training, continued support of an employee's education, and career growth and guidance are a few of the possible ways for a leader to improve as a learner. Leaders who are learners influence employee-students in their intention to stay with their employer and generate direct reductions in turnover and turnover expenses. Employee retention could be improved by increasing either leadership in managers of employee-students or the leadership quality of learner with support and encouragement for an employee's learning, personal growth, and personal development.

Employees who seek a post-secondary degree and utilize tuition reimbursement signal their intention to turnover. Benson et al. (2004) found that employees receiving post-secondary degrees were more likely to leave the company sponsoring their education. Leaders of employee-students must be aware of this *red flag* and must act to identify and retain vital human capital. Understanding employees' intention to turnover can increase employee retention, improve human capital, and reduce losses resulting from turnover.

REFERENCES

Barrett, A., & O'Connell, P. J. (2001). Does training generally work? The returns to in-company training. *Industrial & Labor Relations Review, 54*(3), 647–662.

Becker, G. S. (1975). *Human capital: A theoretical and empirical analysis, with special reference to education* (2nd ed.). New York, NY: National Bureau of Economic Research.

Benson, G. S. (2002). *Beyond skill development: The effects of training and development on the attitudes and retention of employees.* University of Southern California). *ProQuest Dissertations and Theses,* Retrieved from http://search.proquest.com/docview/305515708?account id=35812

Benson, G. S. (2003). Examining employability: Effects of employee development on commitment and intention to turnover. *Academy of Management Proceedings,* C1–C5.

Benson, G. S., Finegold, D., & Mohrman, S. A. (2004). You paid for the skills, now keep them: Tuition reimbursement and voluntary turnover. *Academy of Management Journal, 47*(3), 315–331.

Boggess, S., & Ryan, C. (2002, October). *Financing the future—Postsecondary students, costs, and financial aid: 1996–1997.* Retrieved from http://www.census.gov/prod/2002pubs/p70-83.pdf

Booth, A. L., & Bryan, M. L. (2005). Testing some predictions of human capital theory: New training evidence from Britain. *The Review of Economics and Statistics, 87*(2), 391–394.

Bufe, B., & Murphy, L. (2004). How to keep them once you've got them. *Journal of Accountancy, 198*(6), 57–62.

Daniels, S. (2003). Employee training: A strategic approach to better return on investment. *Journal of Business Strategy, 24*(5), 39–42.

Dillman, D. A. (2007). *Mail and internet surveys: The tailored design method* (2nd ed.). Hoboken, NJ: John Wiley & Sons.

Frank, F. D., Finnegan, R. P., & Taylor, C. R. (2004). The race for talent: Retaining and engaging workers in the 21st century. *Human Resource Planning, 27*(3), 12–25.

Garger, E. M. (1999). Holding on to high performers: A strategic approach to retention. *Compensation & Benefits Management, 15*(4), 10–17.

Glebbeek, A. C., & Bax, E. H. (2004). Is high employee turnover really harmful? An empirical test using company records. *Academy of Management Journal, 47*(2), 277–286.

Gupta, A. (2005). Leadership in a fast-paced world: An interview with Ken Blanchard. *Mid-American Journal of Business, 20*(1), 7–11.

Hacker, C. A. (2003). Turnover: A silent profit killer. *Information Systems Management, 20*(2), 14–18.

Halfond, J. A. (2006). *Smarter tuition-assistance programs: Advice from academe.* Retrieved from http://www.shrm.org/rewards/library_published/benefits/nonIC/CMS_009275.asp

Hersch, J. (1991). Education match and job match. *Review of Economics & Statistics, 73*(1), 140–144.

Koch, W. D. (2006). Better hires, less waste: A potential profit bonanza. *Financial Executive, 22*(4), 29–32.

Loewenstein, M. A., & Spletzer, J. K. (1998). Dividing the costs and returns to general training. *Journal of Labor Economics, 16*(1), 142–171.

McLean, J. (2005). Education: the driving force behind growth and prosperity. *British Journal of Administrative Management, 46,* 18–18.

Miodonski, B. (2005). Re-recruit your best employees to retain them. *Contractor Magazine, 52*(9), 12.

Naude, M., & McCabe, R. (2005). Increasing retention of nursing staff at hospitals: Aspects of management and leadership. *Australian Bulletin of Labour, 31*(4), 426–439.

Neuman, W. L. (2003). *Social research methods: Qualitative and quantitative approaches* (5th ed.). Boston, MA: Pearson Education.

Olesen, M. (1999). What makes employees stay. *Training & Development, 53*(10), 48–52.

Phelan, D. J. (2005). Crossing the generations: Learning to lead across the leadership life cycle. *Community College Journal of Research & Practice, 29*(9/10), 783–792.

Ramsay-Smith, G. (2004). Employee turnover: The real cost. *Strategic HR Review, 3*(4), 7.

Salkind, N. J. (2003). *Exploring research* (5th ed.). Upper Saddle River, NJ: Pearson Education.

Taylor, C. R. (2002). Focus on talent. *T+D, 56,* 26–31.

Thatcher, J. B., Stepina, L. P., & Boyle, R. J. (2002). Turnover of information technology workers: Examining empirically the influence of attitudes, job characteristics, and external markets. *Journal of Management Information Systems, 19*(3), 231–261.

van Breukelen, W., van der Vlist, R., & Steensma, H. (2004). Voluntary employee turnover: Combining variables from the 'traditional' turnover literature with the theory of planned behavior. *Journal of Organizational Behavior, 25*(7), 893–914.

Worster, A., Fan, J., & Ismaila, A. (2007). Understanding linear and logistic regression analyses. *CJEM: The Journal of the Canadian Association of Emergency Physicians, 9*(2), 111–113.

About the Author

Dr. Richard Wolodkowicz is originally from New York, and currently lives in northern New Jersey with his wife and family. Richard holds several accredited degrees; a Bachelor of Science in Mathematics from St. John's University; a Master of Business Administration (M.B.A.) as a dual major in Management and Information Systems from New York University; and a Doctorate of Management (DM) in Organizational Leadership from the University of Phoenix School of Advanced Studies.

As a ground faculty member at the University of Phoenix, Jersey City Campus, Dr. Rich is actively involved in various business courses including Business Communication, Total Quality Management, Business Communication, and Introduction to Research. Additionally, Dr. Rich serves as an adjunct at Ramapo College and has taught Introduction to Information Systems.

Dr. Richard's career spans more than 20 years in information technology and has molded Richard into an accomplished project manager, mentor and coach. Dr. Rich is a transformational leader with strong interpersonal skill, grounded in mentoring and relationship building in a participative style; a communicative, authentic, charismatic, learning leader who uses his knowledge and experience in a corporate environment.

Dr. Richard's published works include his dissertation: *Leadership Qualities and Employee-Student Future Intentions,* and an International Journal of Applied Institutional Governance article entitled, *A Systems Approach to Governance Programs.*

To reach Dr. Richard Wolodkowicz for information on leadership, human resource capital management, coaching, corporate learning initiatives, or any related topics, please visit www.MindBodyGoal.com or e-mail: Richard@Wolodkowicz.com

CHAPTER 8

Assessing for Meaning Out of the Classroom

Dr. Kerry Lynn Levett

Exploring what students learn in college has sparked a revolution in practice within post-secondary education and research that has been fueled by both demands for external accountability and the internal desire to improve the student experience. However, even after several decades of intense scrutiny, clearly discerning the student learning experience remains an enigma for both scholars and practitioners. The elusiveness encompassing student learning in post-secondary environments is partially due to the vast number of variables and combinations of variables that influence student learning, both in aggregate, and at the individual student level. Colleges and universities have engaged in both assessment and research exploring what students are learning. Despite decades of attention from Astin, Kuh, and Associates, Pascarella and Terenzini, little scholarly attention has been paid to what students are learning outside of the classroom in programs, events, and experiences intentionally designed to elicit a learning response from students (ACPA & NASPA, 2004). This chapter will explore how students make meaning of their intentional out-of-class learning experiences by briefly reviewing prominent literature related to the topic, overview a recent study by Levett (2011), and concluding with suggestions for practitioners in post-secondary educational environments.

The 2011 Levett qualitative study explored how students make meaning of their intentional out-of-class learning experiences. The 2011 Levett study is relevant for scholar-practitioners in higher education for two basic reasons. First, external and internal constituencies demand purposeful data collection through both assessment and research (Keeling, 2006). Measures of efficiency and student service access rates are no longer adequate to deem an educational curricular or co-curricular program a success. Second, the assessment movement in higher education has resulted in the use of multiple measures beyond the traditional Grade Point Average (GPA) to determine what students are learning (Keeling, 2006; Love, 1995). The assessment movement includes new measures of student learning that encompasses skills, concepts, and abilities measured in contexts not limited to the classroom (Keeling, 2006). As described by Fried in *Learning Reconsidered 2* (Keeling, 2006), the time has come to pay attention to "our role as learning facilitators," (p.9) and to develop "the language to describe what we are doing in the teaching/learning terminology" (p. 9). Student affairs practitioners have the opportunity to advance the student learning agenda in post-secondary education by actively engaging in assessing student learning outside of the classroom.

Although many higher education professional organizations have called on practitioners to focus on student learning, most of the research centers on discussions of classroom learning. Existing research focused on out-of-class learning continues to target program and functional areas within student affairs such as residence life (Inman & Pascarella, 1997; Pike, Schroeder, & Berry 1997), specific groups such as first generation students (Pascarella, Pierson, Wolniak, & Terenzini, 2004), application of student development theory such as Chickering's vectors (Foubert & Grainger, 2006), and leadership identity development (Komivies, Longerbean, Mainella, Osteen, Owen, & Wagner, 2005). Rather than relying upon frameworks of outcomes and best practices, scholars such as Love (1995) have called for scholarly research into student learning experiences *beyond* the classroom. The goal of the 2011 Levett study was to meet Love's challenge by employing a holistic approach to discovering how students make meaning of what they are learning out of the classroom.

According to Love and Estanek (2004), old paradigms grounded in Newtonian science from over a century ago plague post-secondary education. This dominant worldview limits thinking to *either/or* approaches to experiences. Higher education has been slow to move beyond this traditional thinking. Love and Estanek argued that new science, based in quantum physics, has produced a new paradigm, one that does not replace but coexists with the Newtonian worldview. Simply stated, this new paradigm represents *both/and* rather than *either/or* thinking (Love & Estanek, 2004) which opens the door to exploring intentional students' learning experiences outside of the classroom without dismantling existing research or practice. Rather than maintaining the view that student learning occurs in one or another location, the *both/and* paradigm accommodates student learning which occurs in multiple locations and contacts as a result of a diverse array of experiences. The 2011 Levett study guides student affairs scholar practitioners in interactions with students to create more opportunities for learning in existing programs. Additionally, Levett's study contributes to the on-going process within the student affairs profession to redesign programs and experiences for students that directly target attainment of desired learning outcomes.

Background

As long as higher education has existed, there has been some measure to gauge student learning. Historically, college and university measurement efforts typically involved measures such as GPA and Scholastic Aptitude Test (SAT) scores where content is defined and targeted through classroom teaching activities. Because most student affairs or out-of-class educational activities are not directly linked to course content, surveys on student satisfaction represent the dominate assessment effort to gage the student experience despite the century long urgency to focus on learning. However, as the discussions of assessing student learning continue to expand to multiple contexts, student affairs practitioners are joining in the academic dialog of student learning, thus opening the channel for new research to discover what is happening both inside and outside of the classroom.

Traditionally, cognitive and intellectual development has been the focus of student learning research. In 1996, Terenzini, Pascarella and Blimling summarized the growing body of research tied to out-of-class experiences on learning. They explored student gains from living in residence halls, membership in fraternities and sororities, participating in intercollegiate athletics, on and off campus employment, participating in extracurricular activities, faculty interactions, and peer interactions. Most of the studies they analyzed yielded mixed results for the direct impact of out-of-class educational experiences on cognitive development, especially when viewed as single variables or experiences, confirming that learning is a holistic endeavor. Terenzini, Pascarella and Blimling (1996) identified six conclusions about the impact of out-of-class experiences on student cognitive development, three of which are applicable to understanding the 2011 Levett research:

1. Student affairs programs may not be capitalizing on the potential of students' out-of-class experiences to enhance student learning.

2. The most powerful source of influence on student learning appears to be students' interpersonal interactions, whether with peer or faculty (and, one suspects, staff members).

3. The learning impacts of students' out-of-class experiences are probably cumulative rather than catalytic. (Terenzini, Pascarella & Blimling, 1996, pp. 157–159)

While Terenzini, Pascarella and Blimling (1996) demonstrated the growing evidence for the influence of out-of-class educational experiences on student learning, they also clearly document the gap in research that the 2011 Levett study attempts to bridge.

Another body of research that offers student affairs scholar practitioners an applicable research base on student learning centers on theories of institutional conditions or ethos. In *Involving Colleges*, Kuh, and Associates (1991, 2005) have engaged in numerous research studies detailing institutional variables that contribute to student learning emphasizing learning experiences that occur outside of the classroom. This body of research serves as prominent markers of the institutional ethos approach. Kuh and Associates (1991) identified concrete practices that characterize colleges that try to involve their students including mission and philosophy, campus culture, campus environment, policies and practices, and institutional agents.

Fifteen years later, Kuh et al. (1991) offered another work documented in *Student Success in College: Creating Conditions that Matter* (2005). This work is an outgrowth of the National Survey of Student Engagement (NSSE) research on student engagement drawing upon interviews and conversations with various professionals in higher education through Project DEEP, where DEEP stands for documenting effective educational practice. The purpose of this qualitative case study was "to discover and document the policies, programs, and practices at these [participant] institutions as well as related factors and conditions that were associated with student success" (Kuh et al., 2005, p. 327). The analysis of the massive amounts of data collected yielded what the researchers termed 'guiding principles' as well as recommendations.

Another powerhouse quantitative body of research on the student experience centers on the work of the Higher Education Research Institute (HERI). The Cooperative Institutional Research Program (CIRP) Freshman Survey represents the oldest, most diverse and expansive capture of student educational experiences to date and includes more than 15 million student responses (HERI, 2010). The strengths of the CIRP longitudinal study include capturing a more diverse student experience picture including single administration to both 2- and 4-year colleges, administration of the survey at the start of the student experience typically at orientation programs, a more applicable set of survey questions compared to NSSE including values and attitudes, and trend data dating from 1966 allowing institutions to examine change over the course of time. The outcomes of the CIRP surveys are national norms reports for each year that details aggregate data as well as highlights trends in higher education.

A third type of learning theory body of knowledge applicable to this study is Baxter Magolda's Epistemology Reflection Model (1992, 1995) that described four ways of knowing: absolute, transitional, independent, and contextual (a common post college development). According to Baxter Magolda (1992), students' assumptions about knowing influence their meaning making of experiences both in and out of the classroom. Baxter Magolda (1992) explored how students' out-of-class experiences influenced their development. Student participants defined co-curricular or out-of-class categories as peer relationships, organizational involvement, living arrangements, internship and employment experiences, international experiences, personal changes, and decision-making. For student affairs practitioners to understand student experiences, practitioners must understand students' epistemologies (Baxter Magolda, 1992). Baxter Magolda (1992) concluded this study with a discussion of several areas of co-curricular practice using the challenge-support model of development derived by developmental theorists Piaget and Rodgers (Berger, 2009). By understanding the challenges each type of knower encounters and helping each to build adequate support, offers student affairs scholar practitioners an avenue for impacting student learning and development.

The traditional learning paradigm in higher education asserts that student learning occurs in the classroom, possibly reinforced by educationally purposeful activities linked to class content (Barr & Tagg, 1995; Kuh & Associates, 2005). The direct measures have been traditional course grades or standardized tests. However, the learning paradigm allows for learning to occur in multiple arenas in, around, and connected to the campus (Barr & Tagg, 1995). Planning for and providing student learning no longer belongs only to the academic house, but is a shared responsibility and an obligation for the entire institution. Student affairs professionals are just beginning to understand their functional role in shaping student learning.

Overview of the 2011 Levett Study

The 2011 Levett study followed a qualitative approach to discover meaning tied to a learning experience calls for a qualitative design. Qualitative description is especially appropriate as this study attempted to gain further insight into the multiple year experiences of students rather than a single "snapshot" of college experiences indicative of the predominate research based on survey designs. The site of the 2011 Levett study was a northeastern, private, independent Catholic college, referred to as The College. The College is a relatively young institution located 10 miles south of a metropolitan area, on the edge of the suburban area nestled between a private Catholic girls high school and a convent of the founders of The College.

Based on practical limitations of the research project, the 2011 Levett study employed a purposeful sampling strategy resulting from a list of recommended students demonstrating qualities determined by The College's Vice President to be vital in understanding how students make meaning of their out-of-class educational experience. The initial participant pool included a group of seniors that included The College's Honor Society. Additional criteria were suggested by the Vice President to help identify the final participants who would be able to effectively contribute to this research study. The basic criteria included adequate verbal communication skills, the ability to express personal believes and accurately describe events in his or her life, and campus leadership.

In the course of the interviews the participants described how they became involved in out-of-class experiences and the skills they used to manage their roles. However, the turning points of their experience highlighted how the participants started to make meaning of their out-of-classroom experiences by gaining internal and external understandings of the world around them. For the purposes of the 2011 Levett study, turning points represent moments or experiences that have saliency for the participants, where concepts and ideas meet personal application, where the participants gain understanding of the world in which they live, work and interact with others.

During the data analysis two dimensions of these turning points were delineated from the participants' experiences: external and internal awareness. The external awareness of the participants relates how each participant described how their understanding of others' experiences changed resulting in a shifting of their worldview. For example, one participant, Rachel, described with a sense of awe the affect a hands-on trip had in her understanding of how a small student group could positively impact the lives of those who had been severely traumatized:

> . . . we worked with specific families and worked with the church so we got to know people, um closer. . . . And they were really special to me. I mean the woman sent us a Christmas card later as a thank-you. Um, but I mean it was just, you seen in the news what happened but going there and then listening to their stories about what happened. I mean, the family we worked with, um, the older man was dying and his son and the son's brother in law were there helping, fixing up the house but they had lost everything and we went to where their old house was and they were right by the water. And like just being there and just seeing those little parts like you could see the kitchen floor but there were no walls and it was just really touching and like everybody was just crying. And like you got to see everything first hand and it just made you really realize what we have here and how special it is. Because they lost everything. (Isett-Levett, 2011, pp. 74–75)

Second, the data relating to internal awareness described how the participants began to understand themselves as a result of their out-of-class turning points. Returning to the previous participant, Rachel was the most highly involved of the participants and gravitated towards groups involved in community service. This community service had a huge impact on how Rachel came to be aware of her own privileges:

> My best experience outside of the classroom was when I went and traveled to the Bahamas' or Mississippi or doing the hurricane relief work . . . I mean they were just completely thankful for that and those were the best experiences because it's not something you could've learned, it was just something you . . . you removed yourself from the classroom and learn who you are as a person and those were the best experiences because it showed that I could do that, I could leave home where I have good plumbing and the food that I want and where I have clean clothes, and then you go to a situation like that and you see people so thankful for the smallest things. You learn a lot from that. (Isett-Levett, 2011, p. 82)

Through the interviews, each participant began to gain awareness that their out-of-class experiences have not only had value in terms of acquiring skills, but for understanding the world in which they live, work and interact with others. Hopefully, as the years go by, they will continue to reflect on their experiences to see how the extraordinary opportunities they had impacted them as much as or more than their traditional academic learning.

Limitations

The number of participants in 2011 Levett study was a limitation, as is the homogeneous nature of the participants in terms of their membership in a campus honor society that requires strong academic and out-of-class performance. The emergence of turning points may not be so obvious in students only minimally engaged out of the classroom or lower achieving students. That is an option for further research.

Another limitation was that the campus context was a small, private, religiously affiliated college that not only touted being student-centered, but had such a reputation among prospective students who chose not to attend The College. Consequently, extrapolating the discoveries from this study to another campus, especially a large, research focused institution could yield questions of validity.

Finally, the 2011 Levett study could have been enhanced by employing a longitudinal design, following the participants throughout their time at The College as opposed to collecting data after they had graduated. A longitudinal design could allow for data collection at the specific time a student had an experience as well as after graduation. An alternative design would bring more delineation to the topic, as well as allow the opportunity to engage participants in additional reflection resulting in a clearer picture of how they make meaning of their out-of-class learning experiences.

Findings

The research data indicated that the participants arrived at significant turning points, events that challenged their existing concepts of their realities. The analysis processed involved categorizing turning points as internal or external, differentiating between gains in understanding of self and the world, respectively. These experiences were not necessarily neatly wrapped up in one event, location, or program. Some experiences were sums of events such as athletic participation on multiple teams; others were experiences that took the participants out of their normal comfort zone to a new environment in a foreign country. These were powerful experiences for the participants, powerful enough to impact their worldview and self-understanding, such as when one participant identified a change to how he understands others' personal religious experiences.

Returning to the question of this study of how students make meaning of their out-of-class learning experiences, the simple answer is, students do not necessarily make meaning of out-of-class experiences without some type of processing. However, several important discoveries about students' out-of-class learning resulted from this research. Four of these discoveries will be briefly reviewed.

First, learning is messy, which makes it difficult to research. Most research designs require examining learning from one or a few variables. Researchers have had to narrow projects to a manageable number of variables and control for different contexts to demonstrate some predictive power. However, predicting college student success, such as GPA or time to graduation, continues to baffle most institutions in terms of isolating a specific cause and effect. Learning is not segmented, as demonstrated by the students in this study as well as reflected in *Learning Reconsidered 2* (Keeling, 2006). Perhaps a better model for understanding learning is as a web of interconnected experiences, with occasional breaks in the web. Not every web looks identical, yet yields similar results.

Second, college students lack the appropriate contextual knowledge and language to discuss out-of-class experiences. One participant, Molly, recognized that she had only traditional learning language to discuss her out-of-class experiences, and that perhaps was not adequate. When asked about why she had to think more about her out-of-class experiences compared to her classroom experiences, Molly replied:

> I think because I'm not used to it. I've been in the classroom since of course kindergarten and I think I just became use to it and it became a routine. And I knew exactly what I was doing but with outside of the classroom it's not routine. (Isett-Levett, 2011, pp. 91–92)

The lack of adequate language for students to differentiate multiple learning contexts for students leaves scholars and practitioners in a quandary: How can learning silos be struck down without a common language to integrate the two domains, and yet to create a seamless experience? Furthermore, understanding students' out-of-class learning is limited by students', faculty and staff because the only language used to describe it is from a different context? The student learning assessment movement offers the most practical language bridge at this point.

Third, the variables currently related to impactful student learning, such as the right institutional conditions or the right out-of-class activities, do not necessarily result in students' making meaning of their experiences. Some students are still unsuccessful in our top rated colleges and universities, and students in leadership positions may have visible skills yet lack the ability to work well with those possessing divergent views.

Consequently, and finally, there seems to be a relationship in making meaning of out-of-class and the opportunity to process or reflect on those experiences. The reflective practice is not just a recitation of what the student experienced, but how he or she accommodated the information into his or her own perceptions of the world around him or her. One of the weaknesses of this research design is that the interview process itself engaged the participants in reflective thinking, thus potentially influencing the results.

Implications for Practice

Despite the limitations, the 2011 Levett study highlights the need for making changes in student affairs practice. First, student affairs practitioners need to integrate an opportunity for students to make sense of what he or she experience and learn outside of the classroom, not just for assessment purposes, but as part of an intentional educational process. One of the tangential discoveries of this study was that through the interview process the participants had the opportunity to begin to make meaning of their experiences, thus unlocking previously untapped learning domains resulting from these out-of-class experiences. This previously unexplored learning is related to higher ordered cognitive processes as opposed to basic skills, the types of abilities employers desire in their workers such as multicultural flexibility, problem solving in multiple contexts, and organizational networking (Bresciani, Zelna, & Anderson, 2004). Practitioners can implement reflective practices into daily experiences. For instance, an advisor to a student government association required officers to keep a reflective journal submitted bi-weekly. Simple rubrics have been designed to provide quick feedback to the officers. The journals guide leadership development among the officers as well as help them develop a common set of priorities as a leadership team (Whiffen, personal communication, 2010).

Realistically, incorporating reflective practice is a huge challenge in terms of time and attention of students. The classroom context obviously benefits in having a captured or required audience, unlike out-of-class. However, the assessment movement has provided new tools for practitioners, such as the one minute paper that can be adapted for out of class use. Technology offers unique ways for students to express what they are learning through various forms of media. For example, reports from student organizations or leadership programs could utilize multi-media tools to move beyond regurgitating what was accomplished to include a reflection through pictures, digital images, music, and reflective writing to provide a comprehensive snapshot of what students are learning. The challenge lies in selecting techniques that excite students to engage in these processes by reaching out to their digital world as opposed to traditions of old.

Second, differentiating between learning contexts or environments seems to be a problem when addressing student learning. Keeling (2006) noted that students do not view their learning experiences as segregated silos. Terenzini, Pascarella, and Blimling (1996) affirmed that out-of-class experiences are probably more powerful than most faculty and student affairs staff members realize. Student affairs practitioners need to free learning language from a classroom-only context by incorporating new terms and redefining old ones to help students recognize their significant learning achievements outside of the classroom.

Instead of persisting to define learning in terms of either in-classroom or out-of-classroom contexts, academic and student affairs practitioners need to work collaboratively to advance assessment capabilities to capture learning throughout college as a summative experience as opposed to a segmented one. Educators should encourage students to reflect across their curriculum in the class and beyond. This collaborative, holistic approach is attuned more to the student way of learning and prepares students for merging classroom content, cognitive capabilities, and life management skills to excel in their future endeavors.

Conclusion

The 2011 Levett study focused on exploring how students make meaning of their intentional out-of-class learning experiences. The primary focus of discussion centered on the turning points the student experienced both internal and external. Levett also discovered that the participants rarely had the opportunity to reflect on their co-curricular experiences that may have limited what they ultimately learned from their experiences.

The academic community continues to develop educational programs and activities that attempt to mimic what happens in the co-curricular arena such as service learning, learning communities, and activities day (a unique program at a community college that allows for professors to design special learning opportunities beyond the classroom). The challenge with current collaborations is that because of the dominance of the dualistic, *either/or* model of learning, there is often an imbalance between academic ventures and student affairs. The call to student affair practitioners should not be to collaborate only with faculty more or link engagement in the co-curricular to the curricular, but to create opportunities for students to engage in meaning-making and measure and document their process and progress.

Learning is powerful even without course credit, as demonstrated in this study. The traditional model of higher education continues to revolve around course content at a time when employers are looking for workers not just with content knowledge but also applied knowledge and the ability to transcend multiple contextual environments. The college community lies entrenched in *either/or* thinking where value is college credits or future earnings as opposed to learning for development and improving lifelong abilities (Love & Estanek, 2004). Post-secondary education foundational documents and current research challenge practitioners employ the *both/and* model to provide a more holistic education. Today's scholar-practitioners have a unique opportunity to advance the knowledge and understanding of college students by applying reflective practices and assessment measures to out-of-class educational experiences to demonstrate empirically the value of diverse college experiences for students as they matriculate and as they move into life and employment after their post-secondary education experience.

REFERENCES

American College Personnel Association & National Association of Student Personnel Administrators. (2004). *Learning reconsidered: A campus-wide focus on the student experience.* Washington, DC: authors.

Barr, R. B., & Tagg, J. (1995, November/December). From teaching to learning—A new paradigm for undergraduate education. *Change,* 13–25.

Baxter Magolda, M. B. (1992). Cocurricular influences on college students' intellectual development. *Journal of College Student Development.* (*33*), 203–213.

Baxter Magolda, M. B. (1995). The integration of relational and impersonal knowing in young adults' development. *Journal of College Student Development, 36*(3), 203–216.

Berger, K. S. (2010). *Invitation to the life span,* New York, NY: Worth Publishers.

Bresciani, M. J., Zelna, C. L., & Anderson, J. A. (2004). *Assessing student learning and development: A handbook for practitioners.* Washington, DC: National Association of Student Personnel Administrators.

Foubert, J. D., & Grainger, L. (2006). Effects of membership in clubs and organizations on the psychosocial development of first-year and senior college students. *NASPA Journal, 43,* 166–182.

Inman, P., & Pascarella, E. (1997). The impact of college residence on the development of critical thinking skills in college freshman. *Journal of College Student Development 39*(6), 557–568.

Isett-Levett, K. L. (2011). How students make meaning of their intentional out-of-class educational experiences. (Unpublished doctoral dissertation). Arizona State University, Tempe.

Keeling, R. P. (Ed.). (2006). *Learning reconsidered 2: A practical guide to implementing a campus-wide focus on the student experience.* Washington, DC: authors.

Komivies S. R., Longerbean, D. D., Mainella, F., Osteen, L., Owen, J. E., & Wagner, W. (2005). Leadership identity development: Challenges in applying a developmental model. *Journal of Leadership Education, 8*(1), 11–47.

Kuh, G. D., Kinzie, J., Schuh, J. H., Whitt, E. J., & Associates (2005). *Student success in college*. San Francisco, CA: Jossey-Bass.

Kuh, G., Schuh, J. Whitt, E., & Associates. (1991). *Involving colleges: Successful approaches to fostering student learning and development outside the classroom*. San Francisco, CA: Jossey-Bass.

Love, P. G. (1995). Exploring the impact of student affairs professionals on student outcomes. *Journal of College Student Development, 36*(2), 162–170.

Love, P., & Estanek, S. (2004). *Rethinking student affairs practice*. San Francisco, CA: Jossey-Bass.

Pascarella, E. T., Pierson, C. T., Wolniak, G. C., & Terenzini, P. T. (2004). First Generation college students: Additional evidence on college experiences and outcomes. *The Journal of Higher Education, 75*(3), 249–284.

Pike, G. R., Schroeder, C. C., & Berry, T. R. (1997). Enhancing the educational impact of residence halls: The relationship between residential learning communities and first-year college experiences and persistence. *Journal of College Student Development, 38*, 609–621.

Terenzini, P., Pascarella, E., & Blimling, G. S. (1996). Students' out-of-class experiences and their influence on learning and cognitive development: a literature review. *The Journal of College Student Development, 37*(2).

About the Author

Dr. Kerry Lynn Isett-Levett holds three degrees: a Bachelor's degree from Westminster College (New Wilmington, PA), a Master's for the University of Colorado (Colorado Springs, CO), and a Doctorate of Education from Arizona State University (Tempe, AZ). In addition to doctoral coursework, Dr. Kerry participated in a graduate certificate in institutional research which included completing AIR Institutes in Foundations for the Practice of Institutional Research, and Technology in Institutional Research. Dr. Kerry's career path has included serving local and regional positions for the Presbyterian Church (USA), as well as a full time professor at Cook College & Theological School, a college administrator and adjunct professor (Hilbert College & Finger Lakes Community College), an NCAA Division III softball coach (Hilbert College). Dr. Kerry currently serves as the Associate Vice President of Student Affairs at Finger Lakes Community College (Canandaigua, NY).

Always a student advocate, Dr. Kerry has been passionate about how and what students learn. During her doctorial coursework, she became interested in the power of data to influence the student experience through assessment and research. Dr. Kerry has been a speaker/presenter on applying assessment to student affairs practice as well as student retention.

Presentation & Teaching Interests: student learning experiences & outcomes, assessment/evaluation, research methods, teaching to student learning styles, diversity, retention practices, general student affairs topics, and career pathways in academia.

To contact Dr. Kerry Isett-Levett regarding any of these topics, please email her at kllevett@gmail.com

A Refractive Perspective on Post-Secondary Education and Lifelong Learning

Dr. Tom Woodruff

In the lyrics of a 1966 song, "The 59th Street Bridge Song (Feelin' Groovy)," Simon and Garfunkel suggested that we could be missing opportunities to enjoy life because of our hurried pace. A more relaxed stride might create a more enjoyable environment. While a discussion of song lyrics to start this chapter may seem like an odd introduction to an appraisal of a book dedicated to post-secondary education, the connection might be more realistic than first appearances. Volume VI of the Refractive Thinker® focused on post-secondary education. A variety of refractive perspectives were presented to inform the reader on current concepts in this important arena. The first section of this epilogue exhibits a summary appraisal of the chapters presented. Subsequent sections include a definition of the adult learner, as well as a refractive perspective of the contributions through the lens of sustainable academic leadership and the benefits of lifelong learning.

A Summary Appraisal of Contributions Regarding Post-Secondary Education

Dr. Elena Murphy (2011) initiated this academic effort by

attacking a significant concern in post-secondary education, the retention and graduation of adult learners 25 and older. Murphy noted that the diverse learning styles of adult learners may dramatically affect the retention rate of these learners. Murphy also posited that faculty could determine the learning style preferences of adult learners and could improve success rates by modifying their instructional design. Classroom assessment techniques might also be used to ascertain the progress of adult learners and reduce attrition in the process (Murphy, 2011).

Dr. Denise Land and Dr. Judy Blando (2011) extended the focus on adult learners by illustrating that the use of servant and stewardship leadership practices by faculty members can greatly influence student outcomes. Specifically, Land and Blando concentrated on measurable outcomes for recognized standards in adult learning and noted that a student's mindset may predetermine response to faculty classroom methodology. A key ingredient to successful adult learning in the classroom is the use of practical experience examples that demonstrate and apply theoretical concepts. By identifying the passion of the students, faculty members can modify their instructional design and improve the learning success of their adult learners (Land & Blando, 2011).

Continuing the theme of faculty as a primary factor in adult learners' success, Dr. Rene Contreras (2011) proposed that faculty members have the responsibility to be mentors as well as content experts for their students. While much of the research presented focused on student-teacher mentor relationships in secondary education, Contreras (2011) bridged these concepts to post-secondary educational relationships by demonstrating a similarity between the culture of teachers and leadership development in political constituencies. One key element lacking is mentor training for teachers (Contreras, 2011). Focusing on adult learners underscores the benefits to the student in his or her work environment as a result of mentor relationships with teachers. According to Contreras, adult learners benefit more from mentor relationships than from coaching relationships.

According to Dr. Robert Hobbs (2011), building the foundation for superior performance in post-secondary education starts with the development of multilingual skills in elementary and secondary curricula. Hobbs (2011) portends those students who have not had the opportunity to learn two or more languages at an early age may not develop the same level of cognitive skills as multilingual students. Most of the research cited related to studies in elementary and secondary environments including the potential for more significant academic achievement as a result of increased cognitive skills. The relationship to adult learners may lie in improved communication and metacognitive skills as well as greater tolerance of diversity (Hobbs, 2011).

With a focus on diversity in post-secondary education, Dr. Emad Rahim and Dr. Darrell Burrell (2011) researched negative public perceptions of organizations linked to the term ghetto. These authors examined four community service agencies located in Syracuse, New York. The intention of the study was to provide a causal relationship between negative labels, such as ghetto, and the public perception of the subject organizations. Rahim and Burrell (2011) used the results to develop recommendations to eliminate the negative connotations and to improve public perceptions. The ultimate goal was to develop sustainable improvement measures that may also be relatable to post-secondary education organizations (Rahim & Burrell, 2011).

In the very competitive environment of post-secondary education, Dr. Gillian Silver and Dr. Cheryl Lentz (2011) examined the evolving model of the *consumer learner*. Through the vantage points of administrators, faculty, and students, Silver and Lentz (2011) compared the desires of these three primary components in post-secondary education to assess the current environment. The focus of the administrators has broadened from a quality of education-only perspective to include concerns over sustainability and bottom-line profitability. Consequently, more educational organizations are focusing on the business side of the educational product that they currently offer. The position and focus of faculty has also changed. Instead of judging based on content delivery and student results, faculty members are also reviewed from popularity with students' perspective. As customer service agents, faculty members are often expected to deliver academic content with a focus on the consumer learner. Based on the current price of post-secondary education, the consumer learner is demanding more voice in the process and may want satisfaction guaranteed. These issues suggest a future environment that will need to be both creative and flexible (Silver & Lentz, 2011).

Dr. Richard Wolodkowicz (2011) analyzed the effect that the leadership attributes of employers have on student-employees. Specifically, Wolodkowicz (2011) wanted to determine if these attributes could predict the desire of student-employees to leave the organization after graduation. These same organizations may have paid for some or all of the post-secondary education. According to Wolodkowicz (2011), student-employees who earned a graduate degree were 76% more likely to leave the organization than non-degree employees. As a result of post-secondary education, the performance of student-employees improved along with a desire to pursue other employment opportunities (Wolodkowicz, 2011). While the results of the study did not indicate any significant predictors of student-employee turnover, Wolodkowicz (2011) concluded that student-employees are more likely to stay with organizations in which leaders may also be lifelong learners.

Using the results of a recent study, Dr. Kerry Levett (2011) interpreted the benefits of out-of-classroom experience in post-secondary education. While connecting real world application to classroom theory could be a long-standing tradition at many educational institutions, little research existed that explored the benefits of this experience to the student (Levett, 2011). The primary goal of this study was to assess the meaning of out-of-classroom experience on the student. The implications of the study indicated that incorporating real world applications of the learned theory holds many benefits however this effort also faced significant barriers. Traditional post-secondary educational organizations are hesitant to embrace a scholar-practitioner approach because of the noted challenges. Long-term benefits to the student could far outweigh any short-term pitfalls (Levett, 2011).

This section presented a summary of the offerings in this valuable volume focused on a significant area of education. Some of the presented research emphasized the changing role of faculty and the need to expand established approaches (Fisher-Blando & Land, 2011; Murphy, 2011). Other contributions indicated a connection between elementary and secondary education, and potential success in post-secondary education (Contreras, 2011; Hobbs, 2011). Two chapters considered the effects on students of environmental issues outside of the classroom (Levett, 2011; Rahim & Burrell, 2011). Two more chapters focused on the evolving model of the adult/student consumer and the employee-student in post-secondary education (Silver & Lentz, 2011; Wolodkowicz, 2011). The next section of this epilogue considers a composite view of an adult learner.

A Refractive View of an Adult Learner

Adult learning incorporates the whole person and requires emotional intelligence and spirituality, a learner centered environment, and metacognitive recognition of the influences that created the individual's body of beliefs. A successful adult learning program should revolve around three fundamental components: a) emotional intelligence and spirituality; b) developing the virtual community and learner-centered environment; and c) metacognition and lifelong learning. The following subsections discuss the three elements of this hypothesis and the fourth section summarizes the factors presented; derives conclusions from the material presented, and provides some personal perspectives on adult learning. The analysis begins with an emphasis on the importance of emotional intelligence and spirituality to the adult learner.

Emotional Intelligence and Spirituality

A post-secondary education started for this author immediately after high school. Unfortunately, maturity was not at the level to accept personal responsibility for future education. At the time, no family members had earned a college degree and the influences to pursue this direction were not strong. In many ways this experience underscores the negative perceptions presented by Rahim and Burrell (2011), the lack of a teacher-mentor relationship noted by Contreras (2011), and the cognitive development that may have occurred with multilingual education noted by Hobbs (2011).

After 2 years and 7 months, this author dropped out of college to accept a full-time job. The return to college came over a year later after marriage. In 2 years, a BS degree was earned and 3 years later, an MBA. At the time, the personal vision was that formal education was needed to move beyond blue collar roots and to support wife and children. Merizow (1991) stated that changes in perspective can inspire adults to engage in the pursuit of formal education. Marriage provided the change in perspective for the author. The important reason to establish and pursue long-term personal goals was defined in the presence of married life. Whether this should be described as emotional intelligence or maturity is not important, the important point is that the author chose this direction as a young adult with the support of his wife.

Wlodowski (1998) concluded that the motivation of adult learners who do not earn good grades may decline. The personal experience of the author does not agree with this assessment. The classes taken in the final 2 years of the bachelor degree provided an environment to learn how to become a good student. Grades lower than desired, challenged the author to improve. This took some concerted effort for this individual in his early twenties who wanted to party with friends. With the support of his wife, the author learned to balance these forces and to concentrate on developing the skills needed to succeed as a student. One of the skills enhanced was spirituality.

Tisdell (2008) explained that this type of spirituality is more than just engaging in religion. This type of experience perceives learning on many levels. This spirituality can incorporate conscious learning as well as conceptual subconscious knowledge (Tisdell, 2008). Although religion was one component of this development, the subconscious synthesis of learning in relationship to apparently unrelated segments of life was more significant. These were the seeds that formed the author's attraction to the mystery and complexity of the human brain. The conclusion was and is that our learning capacity is phenomenal. The next subsection considers the virtual community and learner-centered environments that are a critical part of our world.

Developing the Virtual Community and Learner-Centered Environment

Many adults, particularly the Baby Boomer generation, grew up in an environment in which teachers were authority figures to be respected for their education and their positions. Smith (2008) posited that adults view faculty members as experts and creators of knowledge. As an adult who is part of the boomer generation, Smith's premise is accurate from my experience. However as noted in some of the contributions to this volume, the model of the adult student is changing (Silver & Lentz, 2011; Wolodkowicz, 2011).

The author treated teachers throughout his education with respect and believed them to be experts in the subject matter. The respect for professors continued after the return to school to pursue his doctorate degree. The author was out of a formal education environment for 27 years. Even though he was older than many of the professors, he still felt subordinate to them. Part of the system used for the online curriculum required individual as well as team assignments. By emphasizing both, the author became more independent of the professor's knowledge and learned to rely on personal research and the members of his team to promote individual learning. This combination is essential to facilitate adult learning and to build individual confidence (Johnson, 2009; Smith, 2008).

As time and coursework evolved, the author gained more confidence in his ability to perform at a doctoral level. A large part of this confidence came from the growing comfort with the technology of the online environment. Snyder (2009) posited that adult learning can be energized by overcoming any fear of the online technology, by relating the coursework to life experiences, and by requiring different methodologies to produce assignments. This is consistent with the conclusions derived and presented by Murphy (2011) and Fisher-Blando and Land (2011).

Most of the coursework included an emphasis on relating course material to current work environment. These assignments included designing models that used the current work environment as a laboratory. This type of critical and creative thinking promoted the self-direction that Johnson (2009) suggested was a requirement for successful adult learning. The studies presented by Levett (2011) and Wolodkowicz (2011) also noted this same connection. Collectively, these components helped to develop learner-centered goals to become very comfortable and confident in the virtual educational community. The next subsection presents a reflection on adult learners.

Reflection on Adult Learners

The pursuit of knowledge should be a lifelong goal for all adults. Adults are emphasized because many children and teenagers may lack the emotional intelligence or maturity to recognize that learning is a pure goal that can add great value to individual lives. The author did not recognize this value when he first entered post-secondary education. This academic journey is more than just the education required to pursue a professional career. This journey can enhance all levels of an individual's physical and spiritual life.

An important element to adult learners today is developing the technological skills needed to derive knowledge from the many virtual sources available to the educational traveler. A variety of knowledge worlds can be visited simply by driving personal computers through this immense cyberspace of learning. Overcoming any fear of these travels is essential to the success of the adult student. Through this process the adult traveler can develop her or his own virtual community of learners who encourage and support all efforts. This may be the new consumer learner identified by Silver and Lentz (2011).

Beyond these basic principles lies the importance of metacognition that can stimulate our desire and ability to learn and accept new knowledge. According to Pearsall (2009), "there is no end to learning." The author is a firm believer and practitioner of lifelong learning. The intention is to continue learning until the journey ends. The last subsection extends this reflection on metacognition and lifelong learning.

Metacognition and Lifelong Learning

Metacognition in the simplest terms is thinking about thinking. Lifelong learning is self-explanatory. Every adult has a unique toolkit of experience and education that collectively produced the attitudes, beliefs, and approaches he or she has toward the attainment of knowledge (Hofer & Pintrich, 2002; Pintrich, 2002). Much of this knowledge and belief system is entrenched in adult learners and requires a modification of this personal epistemology to open the door to active learning (Murphy & Mason, 2006). Hofer and Pintrich (2002) also maintained that the more knowledgeable and mature an adult is about the beliefs they hold, the more success they will have in educational pursuits. Metacognition is a tool that can be used to expand the use of our brains, to develop our stream of consciousness, to synthesize learning in all aspects of our lives, and to break down perceived physical or spiritual barriers. From a personal perspective, this metacognition effort promotes lifelong learning and the pursuit of knowledge in new directions. Perhaps one might consider this a renaissance in learning!

Conclusion

The purpose of Volume VI of *The Refractive Thinker®* was to take a journey into the world of post-secondary education. The collective effort of this group achieved this goal and added many practical applications and questions to this growing body of knowledge. The authors in this volume succeeded in presenting some illuminating observations on the current state of post-secondary education and potential changes needed to promote success in the future.

As implied by the lyrics of Simon and Garfunkel (1966), we may need to slow our pace and take a concerted view of our educational system as a whole. At times we may change too fast in response to symptoms versus looking deeper at the cause to develop a more permanent cure. Consideration for future research should be given to a second balcony view of our entire educational system to better connect the desired outcomes at the elementary and secondary level to the perceived future objectives at the post-secondary level. Peering down from the second balcony to the dance floor below we may be able to perceive the interactive dance of change as noted by Senge et al. (1999) and become the learning organization (Senge, 2006), which continues to look for avenues of improvement in the post-secondary education system. Our global society continues to evolve and possibly our education system should be restructured to lead this evolution.

As in prior volumes, Dr. Cheryl Lentz provided the refractive environment that allowed this group of authors to perceive a different future in post-secondary education. This was another enjoyable journey to the land of refractive thinking. We hope you enjoyed your reading and will retain this book for future reference. See you in our next publication.

REFERENCES

Contreras, R. H. (2011). Teachers as mentors. In C. Lentz, *The refractive thinker®* (*Volume VI*): *Post-secondary education*. Las Vegas, NV: The Refractive Thinker® Press.

Hobbs, R. D. (2011). Evidence of multilingual superiority: Implications for KG-12 curriculum. In C. Lentz, *The refractive thinker® (Volume VI): Post-secondary education*. Las Vegas, NV: The Refractive Thinker® Press.

Hofer, B. K., & Pintrich, P. R. (Eds.). (2002). *Personal epistemology: The psychology of beliefs about knowledge and knowing*. Mahwah, NJ: L Erlbaum Associates.

Fisher-Blando, J., & Land, D. (2011). Passion: Management behavior to build an engaged learning mindset. In C. Lentz, *The refractive thinker® (Volume VI): Post-secondary education*. Las Vegas, NV: The Refractive Thinker® Press.

Johnson, R. G. (2009). The joys of the journey or "hey, who's in charge here?" *American Music Teacher, 59*, 2, 23–25.

Levett, K. L. (2011). Assessing for meaning out of the classroom. In C. Lentz, *The refractive thinker® (Volume VI): Post-secondary education*. Las Vegas, NV: The Refractive Thinker® Press.

Mezirow, J. (1991). *Transformative dimensions of adult learning*. San Francisco, CA: Jossey-Bass, Inc.

Murphy, E. (2011). Retaining and graduating adult students in higher education: Using learning styles to increase student success. In C. Lentz, *The refractive thinker® (Volume VI): Post-secondary education*. Las Vegas, NV: The Refractive Thinker® Press.

Murphy, P. K., & Mason, L. (2006). Changing knowledge and beliefs. In P. Alexander and P. Winne (Eds.), *Handbook of educational psychology* (2nd ed., pp. 305–324). Mahwah, NJ: Erlbaum.

Pearsall, T. (2009, Oct/Nov). "There is no end to learning": Lifelong education and the joyful learner. *American Music Teacher, 59*, 2, 26–29.
Pintrich, P. R. (2002). The role of metacognitive knowledge in learning, teaching, and assessing. *Theory into Practice. 4(14),* 220–225.

Rahim, E., & Burrell, D. N. (2011). A contextual applied research analysis of negative public perceptions. In C. Lentz, *The refractive thinker® (Volume VI): Post-secondary education.* Las Vegas, NV: The Refractive Thinker® Press.

Senge, P. (2006). *The fifth discipline: The art & practice of the learning organization* (Revised ed.). New York, NY: Doubleday/Currency.

Senge, P., Kleiner, A., Roberts, C., Ross, R., Roth, G., & Smith, B. (1999). *The Dance of change: the challenges of sustaining momentum in learning organizations.* New York: Doubleday/Currency.

Silver, G., & Lentz, C. A. (2011). The consumer learner: Shifts in the teacher/student relationship—Students as customer. In C. Lentz, *The refractive thinker® (Volume VI): Post-secondary education.* Las Vegas, NV: The Refractive Thinker® Press.

Simon, P., & Garfunkel, A. (1966). The 59th street bridge song (feelin' groovy). On Parsley, Sage, Rosemary and Thyme (LP). New York, NY: Columbia Records.

Smith, R. O. (Winter 2008). Adult learning and the emotional self in virtual online contexts. *New Directions for Adult and Continuing Education. 120, 35–43.*

Snyder, M. M. (2009, Jan/Feb). Instructional-design theory to guide the creation of online learning communities for adults. *TechTrends. 53(1),* 45–56.

Tisdell, R. O. (2008, Fall). Spirituality and adult learning. *New Directions for Adult and Continuing Education. 119, 27–36.*

Wlodkowski, R. (1998). *Enhancing adult motivation to learn: A comprehensive guide for teaching all adults.* San Francisco, CA: Jossey-Bass, Inc.

Wolodkowicz, R. (2011). A leader's influence on employee-students seeking post-secondary education. In C. Lentz, *The refractive thinker® (Volume VI): Post-secondary education.* Las Vegas, NV: The Refractive Thinker® Press.

About the Author

Dr. Tom Woodruff and his beautiful wife, Diane, live in Georgetown, Texas. In addition to his most important jobs as husband, father, and grandfather, Dr. Tom serves as Lead Faculty and Area Chair for the School of Business at University of Phoenix-Austin Campus. In addition Dr. Tom is a faculty member with Colorado State University-Global Campus and a contributing faculty member with Walden University. Dr. Tom also serves on the board of The Lentz Leadership Institute.

Dr. Tom holds several nationally accredited degrees including Bachelor of Science in Business Administration, University of Missouri-St. Louis; Master of Business Administration, Southern Illinois University-Edwardsville; and Doctor of Management in Organizational Leadership, University of Phoenix-School of Advanced Studies. He also holds a graduate certificate from SW Graduate School of Banking.

Additional published works include: *Ethical leadership is part of globalization* (2010), *Change agents: Building bridges over resistance* (2009), *Change has no conclusion* (2009), and *Normative leadership types and organizational performance: A case for authoritative performance* (2009).

Index

The
Refractive
Thinker®

and

Pensiero
Press

The Refractive Thinker®:
An Anthology of Higher Learning

The Refractive Thinker® Press
9065 Big Plantation Avenue
Las Vegas, NV 89143-5440 USA

info@refractivethinker.com
www.refractivethinker.com

Books are available through The Refractive Thinker® Press at special discounts for bulk purchases for the purpose of sales promotion, seminar attendance, or educational purposes. Special volumes can be created for specific purposes and to organizational specifications. Orders placed on www.refractivethinker.com for students and military receive a 15% discount. Please contact us for further details.

Refractive Thinker® logo by Joey Root; The Refractive Thinker® Press logo design by Jacqueline Teng, cover design by Peri Poloni-Gabriel, Knockout Design (www.knockoutbooks.com), production by Gary A. Rosenberg (www.garyarosenberg.com).

Pensiero Press

Pensiero Press
9065 Big Plantation Avenue
Las Vegas, NV 89143-5440 USA

> I *think* therefore I am.
> —Renee Descartes
>
> I *critically think* to be.
> I *refractively think* to change the world.

THANK YOU FOR JOINING US as we continue to celebrate the accomplishments of doctoral scholars affiliated with many phenomenal institutions of higher learning. The purpose of the anthology series is to share a glimpse into the scholarly works of participating authors on various subjects.

The Refractive Thinker® serves the tenets of leadership, which is not simply a concept outside of the self, but comes from within, defining our very essence; where the search to define leadership becomes our personal journey, not yet a finite destination.

The Refractive Thinker® is an intimate expression of who we are: the ability to think beyond the traditional boundaries of thinking and critical thinking. Instead of mere reflection and evaluation, one challenges the very boundaries of the constructs itself. If thinking is *inside* the box, and critical thinking is *outside* the box, we add the next step of refractive thinking, *beyond* the box. Perhaps the need exists to dissolve the box completely. As in our first four volumes, the authors within these pages are on a mission to change the world. They are never satisfied or quite content with *what is* or asking *why,* instead these authors intentionally strive to push and test the limits to ask *why not.*

We look forward to your interest in discussing future opportunities. Let our collection of authors continue the journey initiated with Volume I, to which *The Refractive Thinker*® will serve as our guide to future volumes. Come join us in our quest to be refractive thinkers and add your wisdom to the collective. We look forward to your stories.

Please contact The Refractive Thinker® Press for information regarding these authors and the works contained within these pages. Perhaps you or your organization may be looking for an author's expertise to incorporate as part of your annual corporate meetings as a keynote or guest speaker(s), perhaps to offer individual, or group seminars or coaching, or require their expertise as consultants.

Join us on our continuing adventures of *The Refractive Thinker*® where we expand the discussion specifically begun in Volume I with leadership; Volume II with Research Methodology (now in its 2nd Edition); Volume III with Change Management; Volume IV with Ethics, Leadership, and Globalization; and Volume V with Strategy in Innovation—all themed to explore the realm of strategic thought, creativity, and innovation.

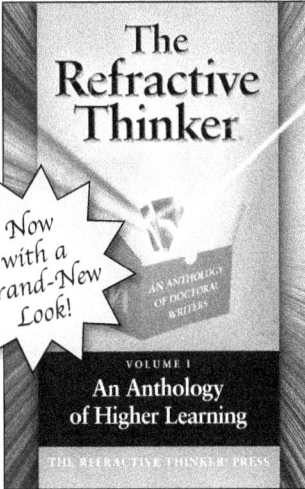

The Refractive Thinker®: Volume I: An Anthology of Higher Learning

The title of this book, *The Refractive Thinker*®, was chosen intentionally to highlight the ability of these doctoral scholars to bend thought, to converge its very essence on the ability to obliquely pass through the perspective of another. The goal is to ask and ponder the right questions; to dare to think differently, to find new applications within unique and cutting-edge dimensions, ultimately to lead where others may follow or to risk forging perhaps an entirely new path.

The Refractive Thinker®: Volume II: Research Methodology, 2nd Edition

As in Volume I, the authors within these pages are on a mission to change the world, never satisfied or quite content with what is or asking *why*, instead these authors intentionally strive to push and test the limits to ask *why not*. *The Refractive Thinker*® is an intimate expression of who we are—the ability to think beyond the traditional boundaries of thinking and critical thinking. Instead of mere reflection and evaluation, one challenges the very boundaries of the constructs itself.

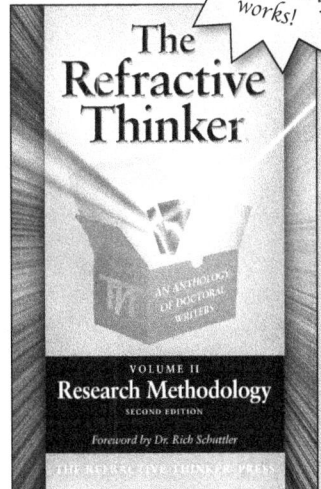

For more information, please visit our website: www.refractivethinker.com

The Refractive Thinker®: Volume III: Change Management

This next offering in the series shares yet another glimpse into the scholarly works of these authors, specifically on the topic of change management. In addition to exploring various aspects of change management, the purpose of *The Refractive Thinker®* is also to serve the tenets of leadership. Leadership is not simply a concept outside of the self, but comes from within, defining our very essence; where the search to define leadership becomes our personal journey, not yet a finite destination.

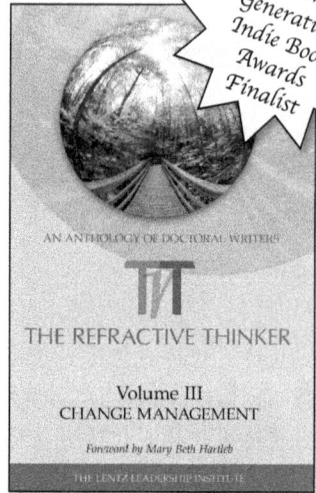

2010 Next Generation Indie Book Awards Finalist

AN ANTHOLOGY OF DOCTORAL WRITERS

THE REFRACTIVE THINKER

Volume III
CHANGE MANAGEMENT

Foreword by Mary Beth Hartleb

THE LENTZ LEADERSHIP INSTITUTE

2011 Next Generation Indie Book Awards Finalist

AN ANTHOLOGY OF DOCTORAL WRITERS

THE REFRACTIVE THINKER

Volume IV
Ethics, Leadership, and Globalization

Foreword by Cam Caldwell, PhD

THE LENTZ LEADERSHIP INSTITUTE

The Refractive Thinker®: Volume IV: Ethics, Leadership, and Globalization

The purpose of this volume is to highlight the scholarly works of these authors on the topics of ethics, leadership, and concerns within the global landscape of business. Join us as we venture forward to showcase the authors of Volume IV, and continue to celebrate the accomplishments of these doctoral scholars affiliated with many phenomenal institutions of higher learning.

Axiom 2011 Bronze Medal • Business Ethics

For more information, please visit our website: www.refractivethinker.com

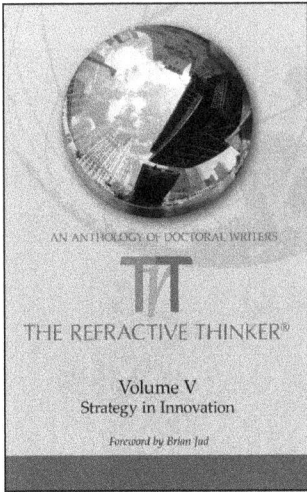

The Refractive Thinker®: Volume V: Strategy in Innovation

Volume V examines the scholarly works of participating authors on the topic of strategic thought in innovation. If thinking is *inside* the box, and critical thinking is *outside* the box, we add the next step of refractive thinking—*beyond* the box. Perhaps the need exists to dissolve the box completely. Our authors are on a mission to change the world, never satisfied with what is or asking *why*, these authors intentionally strive to push and test the limits to ask *why not*.

FROM THE THE LENTZ LEADERSHIP INSTITUTE

Journey Outside the Golden Palace

Come take a mythical journey with Henry from *The Village of Yore* and the many colorful characters of The Golden Palace on their quest to unlock the palatial gates of corporate Ivory Towers. This allegorical tale demonstrates the lessons learned when leaders in organizations fail to serve the needs of their stakeholders. Come join us in a journey toward understanding the elegant simplicity of effective leadership, unlocking the secrets to The Golden Palace Theory of Management along the way.

This revised second edition offers a companion workbook for discussion, reflection, and refractive thinking. The purpose of this workbook is to more closely examine each character and their leadership qualities. Take a leap of faith and follow us on our journey. Perhaps you may recognize some old friends on your travels.

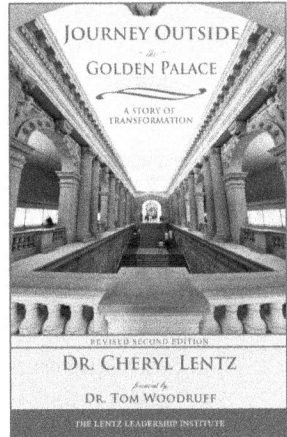

Pensiero Press TO PUBLISH LANDMARK BOOK ON CHANGING ADULT EDUCATION ARENA

DECEMBER 1, 2011, LAS VEGAS, NV—Anyone who has entered a college classroom in the last 5 years has recognized a clear transformation in the context of higher education. A dynamic revolution in practice and delivery is underway, and the implications of multi-faceted change are ripe for analysis.

Administrators are increasingly charged with revenue production and institutional leadership. Faculty are experimenting with new andragogical models and advances in interactive technology. Students are embracing new modalities, as they strive to make curriculum immediately transferable into industry. *The Consumer Learner: Emergence and Expectations of a Customer Service Mentality in Post-Secondary Education* examines the new reality and emerging patterns shaping the experiences of these three diverse, yet interconnected, constituencies.

THE

CONSUMER LEARNER

Emerging Expectations of a Customer Service Mentality in Post-Secondary Education

DR. GILLIAN SILVER AND DR. CHERYL A. LENTZ

This book provides a distinctive approach to the transformation of the higher education culture within the United States. Authors Dr. Gillian Silver and Dr. Cheryl Lentz, noted content experts, professors and curriculum/program developers, explain that the contents will initiate an intensive dialogue about the implications and impacts on administrative structure, faculty practice, and learner outcomes. According to Dr. Lentz, "This is a frank, encompassing work which has the capacity to ignite a national dialogue. We think the review will give voice to the significance of this evolving environment. The voices of experience leading this change will emerge."

The Consumer Learner: Emerging Expectations of a Customer Service Mentality in Post-Secondary Education will be issued by Pensiero Press, a division of the The Lentz Leadership Institute, in Winter 2011. Preorders are available from our website at the pre-publication price of $16.95 for the first release in hardcover. Retail: $24.95

Follow the authors on the Web: www.consumerlearner.com
and Blog: www.consumerlearner.com/wordpress/

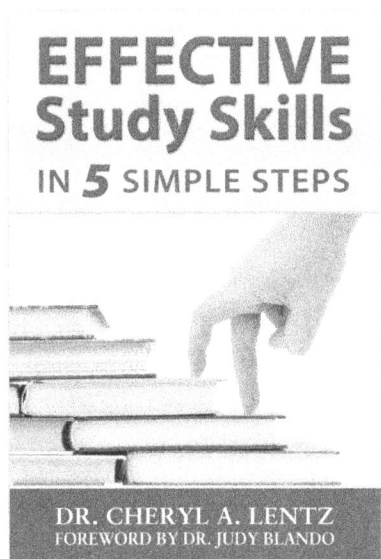

EFFECTIVE
Study Skills
IN **5** SIMPLE STEPS

Dr. Cheryl Lentz has compiled the valuable information she gives in her blog in one easy-to-use handbook. The study tips are designed to help any student improve learning and understanding, and ultimately earn higher grades. The handbook is not so large that it requires long hours of reading, as is the case with many books on the subject. The information is written in a manner to help a learner "see" and "practice" proven study techniques. Effective study skills must be practiced to for improvement to occur.

PUBLICATIONS ORDER FORM

Please send the following books:

❏ *The Refractive Thinker®: Volume I: An Anthology of Higher Learning*

❏ *The Refractive Thinker®: Volume II: Research Methodology*

❏ *The Refractive Thinker®: Volume II: Research Methodology, 2nd Edition*

❏ *The Refractive Thinker®: Volume III: Change Management*

❏ *The Refractive Thinker®: Volume IV: Ethics, Leadership, and Globalization*

❏ *The Refractive Thinker®: Volume V: Strategy in Innovation*

Please contact the Refractive Thinker® Press for book prices, e-book prices, and shipping.
Individual e-chapters available by author: $3.95 (plus applicable tax). www.refractivethinker.com

❏ *The Consumer Learner: Emergence and Expectations of a Customer Service Mentality in Post-Secondary Education*

❏ *Effective Study Skills in 5 Simple Steps*

❏ *Journey Outside the Golden Palace*

Please send more FREE information:

❏ Speaking engagements   ❏ Educational seminars   ❏ Consulting

Join our Mailing List

Name: _____

Address: _____

City: _____ State: _____ Zip: _____

Telephone: _____ Email: _____

Sales tax: NV Residents please add 8.1% sales tax

Shipping: *Please see our website for shipping rates.*

Please mail or fax form to:

The Refractive Thinker® Press/
  Pensiero Press
9065 Big Plantation Ave.
Las Vegas, NV 89143-5440 USA
Fax: 877 298-5172

Participation in
Future Volumes of
The Refractive Thinker®

Yes, I would like to participate in:

❏ **Doctoral Volume**(s) for a specific university or organization:

Name: _____

Contact Person: _____

Telephone:_____ E-mail: _____

❏ **Specialized Volume**(s) Business or Themed:

Name: _____

Contact Person: _____

Telephone:_____ E-mail: _____

Please mail or fax form to:

The Refractive Thinker® Press
9065 Big Plantation Ave.
Las Vegas, NV 89143-5440 USA
Fax: 877 298-5172
www.refractivethinker.com

Join us on Twitter, LinkedIn, and Facebook

213

www.ingramcontent.com/pod-product-compliance
Lightning Source LLC
Chambersburg PA
CBHW060552220326
41598CB00024B/3077